THE
COUNTRY FAIR
CRAFT BOOK

by

ALISON BOTELER

To My Mother . . .
many thanks for encouraging this whole concept.
You help me see the potential in anything and everything.

• • •

To Mary Beth . . .
I hope this book gives you and Thomas many hours
of entertaining projects in the years to come.

Copyright © 1995 Alison Boteler

All inquiries should be addressed to:
Barron's Educational Series, Inc.
250 Wireless Boulevard
Hauppauge, NY 11788-3917

Library of Congress Catalog No. 94-40846

ISBN 0-8120-6439-9

Library of Congress Cataloging-in-Publication Data
Boteler, Alison Molinare.
 The country fair craft book / by Alison Boteler.
  p. cm.
  ISBN 0-8120-6439-9
  1. Handicraft.   I. Title.
TT157.B693 1995
745.5—dc20   94-40846
                                              CIP

PRINTED IN HONG KONG
5678   9927   987654321

THE COUNTRY FAIR CRAFT BOOK

❖

INTRODUCTION

❖

In this mass-produced, disposable world we live in, many are looking for something more. They're looking for quality and a special connection that only comes from buying handmade goods and meeting the maker. This is what country fairs, craft shows, and holiday bazaars are all about. Our forefathers went to country fairs and markets to make seasonal purchases for the home and family. They knew they could depend on the same regional vendors to be there year after year. They knew they could depend on their workmanship and reputation. From children's toys to harvest tables, they knew they could be proud of their unique purchase. There was no other exactly like it.

In recent years such fairs are again becoming a national pastime. From small towns to city suburbs, "country craft fairs" are cropping up everywhere, a recreational sport for both collector and crafter. They bring communities closer together while creating a common bond between people who share the same interests. They raise money for worthy causes as people contribute their time and talent. They also provide a wonderful social outlet. People meet their neighbors at these events while making new friends as well.

This book was created to bring some of those country fair crafts into your home. The projects are simple and the instructions are easy to follow. Step-by-step drawings and patterns will help guide you along the way. You won't need specialty skills or expensive tools; all you need is a love for handcrafted quality. Experience the rewards by experiencing the process. Once you get started, you just can't stop!

❖   ❖   ❖   ❖

CRAFTING BASICS FOR BASIC CRAFTS

❖

E*very craft project has its own unique list of materials, much as a recipe requires specific ingredients. It would be impossible to stock your kitchen with all the perishables or seasonal foods called for in your favorite cookbook—but it's wise to have an intelligently stocked pantry of staples. Having certain basic equipment and craft supplies in your home makes similar sense. I've excluded projects requiring knitting, crocheting, and needlework; these skills call for entire books unto themselves and can be intimidating to the untrained. Likewise, woodworking projects that involve expensive (and potentially dangerous) power tools are not an option for many readers. However, most households have a sewing machine. It may be frequently used or collecting dust in the guest room closet, but chances are, you know how to make it "go"! The following tools and techniques are those most essential to this book.*

❖

PRECISION PATTERNS

The majority of craft projects involve the use of some sort of pattern. Whether you're cutting wool or wood, you'll need to transfer the design onto the material's surface. Often it must first be enlarged to scale, using a grid of squares representing a unit of measurement that is usually larger (but sometimes the same) in size. The simplest way to copy patterns of the same scale, or of an enlarged size up to $8^{1}/_{2}$ inches $\times$ 11 inches, is to use a photocopying machine. If the pattern is larger than the paper allows, it can be pieced together in sections. The more traditional (and time-consuming) method involves making your own grid to scale. For example, if $^{1}/_{4}$ inch =1 inch, you'd use a yardstick and a roll of paper to make a grid of 1 inch squares large enough for the finished pattern. You would follow the lines of the smaller pattern onto the larger grid, making your own freehand copy. (This is how billboard artists used to paint signs.) A wonderfully clever, relatively inexpensive device is a pattern enlarger, which works the same way as one of those overhead projectors used in schools. Tape a sheet of paper to the wall and you can enlarge a postage stamp to the size of a poster! The image is easy to trace. (By the way, this is a neat trick if you ever want to attempt a mural.)

Sometimes it's also necessary to transfer the lines of the pattern directly onto fabric or another surface. If you can't cut or draw around a pattern shape, you can try tracing paper, a type of colored transfer paper used for dressmaking. It's less messy than typewriter carbon paper, and much larger. Another way is to use a lead pencil. No, I don't mean rubbing all over the back of a paper the way you might have learned as a child—there's a cleaner way. Copy your pattern (enlarged if necessary) onto a fairly sheer sheet of paper with a red ink marker. Turn it over and trace the exact lines on the reverse side with a carbon pencil (pattern will be backward). Turn paper right side up against the surface you wish to mark and draw over the red lines with a blue pencil. (If marking fabric, be sure it's against a hard tabletop.) The blue pencil helps remind you of which lines you've covered.

❖

PAINT BOX

The projects in this book generally call for water-based products. Even wood stains can now be found in water-based formulas. I simply find no reason to contend with fumes or a major cleanup operation unless absolutely necessary—and your paintbrushes will last longer. Acrylic paints come in tubes and bottles; fabric paints are acrylics that dry with more flexibility and durability. (These can usually be washed but often require setting the paint with a hot iron.) Use 1- to 1¹/₂-inch flat brushes or sponge-stick applicators for covering large areas. Tapered detail brushes and felt markers are necessary for more intricate work. Natural sponges are useful for applying paint with a feathery effect. Dimensional paints are piped directly from tubes to create a raised relief. Stencil paints now come in thick paste form, similar to lip gloss; they are applied with round, stubby stencil brushes. Leaves, sliced fruit, and other objects can be used to stamp impressions on surfaces. Aluminum pie pans make great paint palettes for this process. Aluminum foil *makes a better drop cloth than newspaper. Most projects need a finishing coat of brush-on or spray acrylic sealer. These come in matte or gloss; in most cases a natural matte finish is the best choice.*

❖

SEWING BASKET

When was the last time you used your sewing machine? Chances are you made a ridiculous bridesmaid's dress or a Halloween costume. Well, it's time to dust that machine off. In addition to traditional home decorating crafts, you can use it to make anything from dolls to soft sculpture. A sewing machine is simple to master and a valuable tool. There's no need to buy a top of the line, computerized model. (Believe me, I have one and I haven't touched most of the dials.) A standard straight stitch (for sewing and basting) and a zigzag (for overcasting and appliqué) are all you really need. A buttonhole feature or attachment is a major plus but not essential; you can easily make buttonholes using a simple satin stitch. If you don't want to invest in a sewing machine, you probably have several friends or relatives who keep one up in their attic. Borrow it or, better yet, trade it for one of the craft projects you're about to produce.

*Some situations call for hand sewing. That's because your fingers can go where a presser foot can't. Generally craft projects sewn by machine have a $^1/4$- to $^1/2$-inch seam allowance; the seams are clipped around the curves and corners, and then pressed open. Sometimes the project is too small or the seam allowance is too narrow to do this. That's when you use a technique called **whipstitching,** a method of join-*

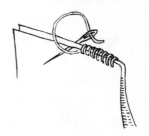

ing two pieces of fabric with a narrow hand stitch. The stitches are made close together, to a depth of about $^1/2$ inch from the edges of the fabric. As each stitch is sewn, you "whip" around the edges of the fabric in an overcast stitch (Fig. 1).

Fig. 1

Slipstitching is another important technique; it's used to close up a turning hole or the side seam of a stuffed toy. You join the two folded-under edges of fabric from the right side of the fabric, pricking the needle through the folded edge of each side in alternating stitches. The objective is to keep the running thread hidden inside the folds (Fig. 2).

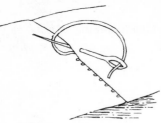

Fig. 2

Finally, if you don't want to use a sewing machine, you can join long, major seams with a **chain stitch.** (Before the industrial revolution, that's how clothing was made.) A stitch about 3/16 inch long is made through two pieces of fabric. The needle is then brought back halfway through the stitch before moving on to the next stitch (Fig. 3). Seams made in this fashion can be pressed open in the same way as those made by machine.

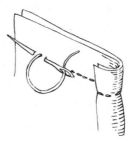

Fig. 3

Be sure to keep the following sewing staples in some kind of kit or basket: assorted needles and pins, pincushion, seam gauge, tape measure, tailor's chalk or pencil, a good pair of scissors, and pinking shears. (Don't dull the sharp edges of your scissors by using them to cut anything other than fabric.)

❖

WORKBENCH

As I mentioned earlier, there's no need to be intimidated by basic woodcraft projects. You do not need a collection of pricey power tools; any tools required in this book are probably around your house. If they're not, you should own them for your own simple home repairs. Let's start with the basics: hammer, tack hammer, pliers, screwdriver, and a vise to hold wood. You should also have three types of cutting tools: a regular crosscut saw, a scroll saw (or coping saw) with blades, and a craft knife with both straight and serrated blades. For making small holes you'll need a hand drill with assorted bits. For larger holes (from 3/8 inch to 1 inch) an auger and a set of auger bits will work just fine. Be sure to keep an assortment of screws, sandpaper, wire, and finishing nails on hand.

❖
HOLD IT!

Know your glue. Using the right product for the right purpose is essential to crafting success. Familiarize yourself with the unique properties of different glue types. When you shop for project materials, don't deviate from the suggested adhesive.

***Thick craft glue** is the gold standard of glue. It sets up quickly without drying completely— a real advantage when you're working slowly. Some of the latest formulas bond as well as hot glue guns, without the hassle. Whenever I have the choice, I prefer a powerful craft glue to a glue gun; the craft glue gives you time to change your mind.*

***Hot glue guns** are a major rage, and for a good reason: they instantly bond relatively heavy objects to other objects. There's no waiting to dry or watching things fall off. However, the guns have some serious drawbacks. First of all, you have to work fast. The glue hardens in a matter of seconds, often spinning threads of glue from the gun to your project. Sometimes the glue hardens before you have a chance to bond it to a surface. You need to plan your moves carefully because once you start, there's no time to think! Glue guns are also messy, but some of the mess can be avoided by investing in a large gun with a trigger. Large guns use larger glue sticks. You won't waste time stopping to change sticks every other minute, which also wastes glue. A trigger is a must (many small, inexpensive guns don't have this feature)— it helps control the flow of glue. Which brings me to a final point about glue guns: they can burn your fingertips. Low-melt glues are much easier to tolerate than the hot-melt variety. Each type requires its own set of sticks, since they liquefy at different temperatures. I always keep a "first aid" dish of ice water next to me when using a glue gun.*

***Epoxy and super bonding glues** are the only choice for fusing certain materials: metal to metal, glass to glass, glass to metal, stone to stone. Generally hard, slick surfaces require this type of bond. Epoxy is strong but does not set instantly. It is typically a two-part product that is mixed immediately before application. Newer products come in dual dispensers whose contents combine as you squeeze the tube. Epoxy emits fumes and should only be used by adults or under adult supervision. Similarly, super bonding glue is not child's play.*

Who hasn't fastened a couple of fingers together with this product? Still, it has its advantages, and it sets almost instantly. Newer formulas and improved dispensers have addressed some of the typical problems.

Fabric glue is a product that remains flexible once it dries. Many brands are durable enough to survive the laundry. Check the labels of specific products to see which best suits your needs.

Acrylic polymer is almost universally known as Modge Podge®. It was introduced decades ago as a decoupage medium. This is a wonderful adhesive, topcoat, and glaze. The water-based formula cleans off a brush with warm water and comes in matte or gloss finish.

Wood glue is one of the oldest glue products, historically used by carpenters for fine furniture joinery. It's still the preferred adhesive for woodcrafts. The glue sets slowly and usually needs to be held in place in a vise or clamps, or with nails.

Gesso really isn't a glue as much as it is a sealant to prepare surfaces for paint. When applied to figures sewn from fabric, it practically turns them into hard sculpture. The first coat of gesso needs to be painted on with a very damp sponge to saturate the fabric fibers. Repeated coats go on with a drier sponge. Gesso should be lightly sanded between coats for a smooth, paintable finish.

Napkin appliqué glue is an intriguing new product that allows you to cut designs from paper napkins and fuse them to permanent surfaces. The end result is flexible enough to apply to fabric and canvas. It also works well on woven straw and wood.

Glue sticks come in regular and temporary bond. Those designed for fabric make sewing projects easier. The glue stick tacks appliqués in place without pins or basting stitches. Temporary-bond glue sticks make paper removable, much like a Post-it® note.

Fusible web bonds fabric to fabric with the heat of an iron. It can sometimes replace sewing in a project and it makes appliqué much easier.

Setting Up Shop

❖

Whether you're making one doll for your daughter or mass-producing dozens for a community bazaar, your materials are of utmost importance. Expense is not a measure of quality. Many of the most creative crafts are made with elements borrowed from nature—seashells, pinecones, branches, twigs, nuts, berries, dried flowers and fruits, just to name a few. Old-fashioned fabrics like muslin and homespun have more charm than printed "craft fabrics" sold by many fabric store chains. Sometimes the most obvious, simple objects make the most interesting crafts, like a bottle wrapped in manila rope or a sock sewn up like a snowman. It's the concept that counts.

If you're working with an organization, such as a school or church committee, you might consider pooling skills and supplies. Find out where each individual's talent lies. Some are better at building bird feeders; some excel at painting them. Some materials, like cotton or polyester stuffing, are simply cheaper in bulk. Fabrics have a better price per yard if purchased by the bolt. With some other materials there are simply no bargains. This is particularly true of patented paint and specialty glue products; whether you're buying one tube or twenty tubes, there's no price break. Most of the sources for these supplies are large craft chains and small hobby shops. I've noticed little difference in prices between the two. The best way to find a bargain is to sign up for sale flyers, which will bring discount coupons right to your house. Buy ribbon by the bolt on sale days; when you consider the price per yard, I save a bundle. As for lumber, small lumberyards and hardware stores are giving way to home improvement centers, and you can't beat their prices on most building materials.

Perhaps you simply want to start your own hobby/business exhibiting at craft shows. There are plenty of opportunities. Country fairs and craft bazaars abound in most areas, rural and suburban. Check your local paper for announcements and entry requirements or look in craft magazines. Creating crafts to sell can mean big business!

❖   ❖   ❖   ❖

SPRING

❖

Spring is the awakening of our senses. Floral fragrances fill the air, and green thumbs begin planting for the summer and fall harvests. Major state fairs and county festivals are still in the making for the seasons to come. Now is the time for local country bazaars and craft and flower shows. Many community events revolve around designer showcase homes and garden club tours. Homeowners have traditionally looked to these shows for inspiration. Depending on the area where you live, you can look forward to Dogwood Festivals, Jonquil Jubilees, or Azalea Trails. Crafts featured at these affairs usually reflect spring holidays: St. Patrick's Day, Easter, May Day, and Mother's Day. Along with shamrock sachets, stuffed bunny dolls and May baskets, expect to find home accessories, floral wreaths, and shower gifts. Many spring fabric projects require a sewing machine. Other crafts and decorative arts can easily be merged with a simple needle and thread, hammer and nail, or a hot glue gun.

SPRING

❖

St. Patrick's Day Scented Shamrocks

Lavender-Mint Potpourri

Pansy Pots

Shaker String Easter Eggs

Robin's Egg Nests

Benjamin Bunny Doll

Bo Peep Puppet

Appliqué Bonnet

May Day Nosegay Wreath

Scissors Doll in Sponge-Painted Sewing Kit

Raggedy Wrapped Rope Basket

Bow Pillow

Hospitality Luminary

Crazy Caterpillar

St. Patrick's Day Scented Shamrocks
Makes 4

❖

*T*hese delicate shamrocks are stitched together out of Irish linen and lace, then stuffed with lavender-mint sachet. Tuck these away with those winter wool sweaters, and they'll stay fresh as an Irish spring!

1/4 yard green linen
1/4 yard (or less) crocheted lace fabric
3/4 yard 1/2-inch green satin ribbon
pins
scissors
needle
thread (to match linen)
Lavender-Mint Potpourri
(instructions follow)

Cut 8 shamrock shapes from linen, using pattern. Cut 4 more shamrocks from crocheted lace fabric. For each sachet: place lace over right side of one linen shamrock (Fig. 1), lining up so edges are even. Cut 6-inch length of ribbon and fold into a 3-inch loop. Position loop at base of shamrock, facing in (Fig. 2); this will form a stem when turned. Pin second linen shamrock to lace, right side down. Stitch around fabric 1/4 inch from edge, leaving an opening to turn. (Fig. 3).

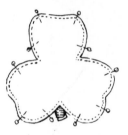

Fig. 3

Trim seam allowance close to stitching line. Turn shamrock right side out and press. Stuff with potpourri and slipstitch opening (Fig. 4).

Fig. 4

(Continued)

Fig. 1

Fig. 2

Opposite: Benjamin Bunny Doll, page 10
Preceeding Page: St. Patrick's Day Scented Shamrocks, page 3
With Lavender-Mint Potpourri, page 5

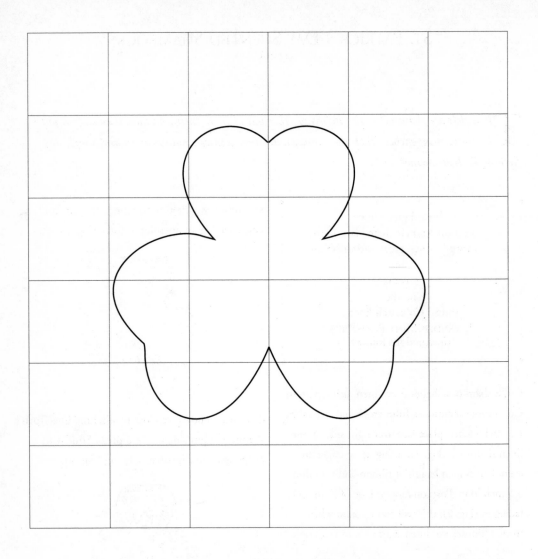

1 square = 1 inch

LAVENDER-MINT POTPOURRI
MAKES ABOUT 2 3/4 CUPS

2 cups dried lavender petals
2 dozen eucalyptus leaves, crushed
1/4 cup dried mint, crushed
1/4 cup dried rosemary, crushed
1 teaspoon orrisroot powder*
4 to 5 drops concentrated lavender oil

Toss together and store in airtight jar or container.
Makes enough to fill about 8 to 10 shamrocks.

NOTE: Look for orrisroot powder at a nursery
crafts store or in the floral department of a
supermarket.

PANSY POTS
MAKES 4

❖

Pansies are like people: each one has a unique expression. Unlike people, you don't need a camera to capture the moment. The delicate blossoms can be pressed between sheets of waxed paper and preserved for posterity. Rather than display them in frames, I like to decoupage them onto flower pots (the perfect setting for pansy sets!)

2 dozen pansy blossoms and leaves
waxed paper
heavy books
four 4-inch clay pots
Seafoam green acrylic paint
natural sponge
matte acrylic polymer
sponge-tip paint applicator
potting soil
pansy sets

Carefully place pansy blossoms and leaves between sheets of waxed paper. Press between heavy books until flowers are dry (about 2 to 3 weeks). Generously "blot" green paint on the surface of pots with a natural sponge, allowing some of the clay to show through. When paint is dry, brush polymer on the areas where you want to apply the pansy blossoms and leaves. Gently press blossoms and leaves onto pot. (Be careful; they're fragile.) Once dry, gently cover the entire surface of the pots (including flowers) with two coats of polymer, allowing to dry between coats. Fill with potting soil and plant sets of pansies.

SHAKER STRING EASTER EGGS
MAKES 12

———— ❖ ————

*S*tring-wrapped eggs are among America's oldest craft items. They served as tree ornaments during the Christmas holidays and lined Easter baskets in the spring. These are elegantly displayed when piled into a simple Shaker box. Thanks to improved craft glues, they're easier than ever to make. If blowing raw eggs bothers your eardrums, buy the styrofoam version from a crafts store.

> 1 dozen raw eggs (or styrofoam eggs)
> embroidery needle
> paintbrush
> thick craft glue
> cotton string or yarn in a combination
> of pastel or colonial colors

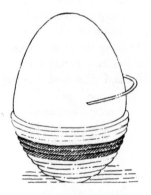

Fig. 1

To blow raw eggs: pierce egg at both ends with needle. Hold narrow end over bowl and blow at large end until contents of egg are completely emptied. Allow egg to dry for 24 hours. To wrap eggs: brush small amount of glue at one end and begin winding string around egg. Keep rows of string tightly wrapped so none of the eggshell shows through (Fig. 1).

Continue to add glue as you work around egg. Eggs may be solid, parti-colored, or striped. To change colors, cut string and pick up where you left off with a new color (Fig. 2). Allow eggs to dry at least 4 hours.

Fig. 2

ROBIN'S EGG NESTS
MAKES 12

❖

These fragile ornaments are quite striking when displayed in a natural grapevine basket lined with moss. Inside each delicate blue eggshell is a baby bird made from bread dough. I've kept mine on the dining room table, long after the Easter baskets have gone into storage.

1 dozen raw jumbo eggs
sharp serrated knife
embroidery needle
1 tablespoon white vinegar
1 1/2 cups boiling water
blue and green food coloring
plastic glove
2 slices white bread
1 tablespoon cocoa
Popsicle stick
thick craft glue
1 dozen toasted almond slivers*
2 dozen whole cloves
Spanish moss
grapevine basket (optional)

Hold each egg over bowl and poke hole in side with embroidery needle. Carefully work tip of knife into hole, cutting out jagged opening in side of egg. (Be careful not to break egg. Opening should be about 1 1/2 inches across.) Empty contents of egg into bowl. Rinse eggshells and allow to dry.

Combine vinegar, water, and several drops each blue and green food coloring in small, deep bowl (try to achieve the color of "robin's egg blue"). Hollow eggshells are fragile, so it's best to dye them individually by hand, using a plastic glove. One by one, immerse eggshells in dye. Allow cavity to fill with dye so egg sinks. When eggshell has absorbed enough color, remove from bowl, pouring dye in cavity back into bowl. Allow to dry 24 hours in egg carton.

Meanwhile, prepare baby birds. Discard crusts from bread and tear bread into very fine pieces. Combine bread crumbs with cocoa in small bowl. Add about 2 tablespoons glue and mix with Popsicle stick until ball forms. Knead dough in hands until very smooth, about 10 minutes. Shape dough into balls: 12 that are about 1/2 inch to 5/8 inch in diameter, and 12 that are about 5/8 inch to 3/4 inch in diameter. Place small balls on top of larger ones (Fig. 1).

NOTE: Toast almonds in 375° (190°C) oven for 5 to 10 minutes, stirring 3 times while baking.

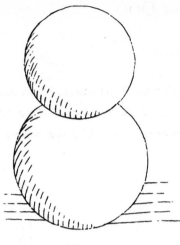

Fig. 1

Carefully glue small amount of moss in bottom of each egg to resemble nest. Glue baby bird inside nest, taking care not to break shell (Fig. 3). If desired, line natural grapevine basket with additional moss and arrange eggs in basket for display.

Contour balls slightly. Insert almond sliver for beak and cloves for eyes (Fig. 2). Allow to dry thoroughly. Birds will shrink somewhat, depending on brand of bread.

Fig. 3

Fig. 2

Benjamin Bunny Doll
MAKES 1

❖

*H*ere's a spring bazaar item that's just perfect for stuffing into Easter baskets. Floppy-eared rabbits seem to multiply at country fairs and are probably the most popular doll there. Some complex bunny bodies can have as many as 16 pattern pieces, but this simple 4-piece version is easy enough for beginners to make.

1/4 yard natural muslin
pins
scissors
needle
thread (to match muslin and felt)
pink pencil
cotton or polyester stuffing
two 1/4-inch black shoe buttons
pink embroidery floss
9-inch × 12-inch square of blue felt
two 1/4 inch brass buttons
ball fringe pom-pom

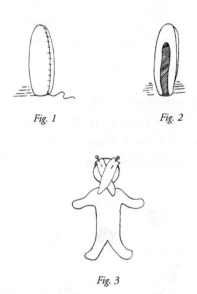

Fig. 1   Fig. 2

Fig. 3

Enlarge patterns to scale. Cut 2 pieces from body pattern and 4 pieces from ear pattern, using muslin. Whipstitch 2 ear pieces together around edges, right sides together, and turn inside out (Fig. 1).

Repeat with remaining 2 ear pieces. Press flat and shade inside of each ear with pink pencil (Fig. 2).

Pinch base of ears together, folding in half, and pin to body section as shown (Fig. 3).

Baste in place. Pin remaining body section over ears and whipstitch about 1/8 inch from edge, leaving space to turn (Fig. 4).

Turn bunny right side out and fill with stuffing. (Do not close opening before stitching on face. You may need to push your finger inside head to

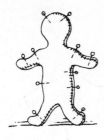

Fig. 4

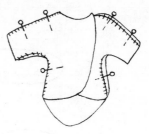

Fig. 6

adjust stuffing.) Make eyes by sewing shoe buttons on face about 1 inch apart, connecting thread between eyes inside head. Stitch nose and mouth with pink embroidery floss. Shade top of nose in inverted triangle with pink pencil. Add more stuffing if necessary and slipstitch opening (Fig. 5).

Turn; press down lapels. (You may use a few hidden stitches to anchor lapels in place.) Cut slash in back for vent. Slip jacket onto body and overlap in front. Secure jacket by sewing on brass buttons through both layers of felt (Fig. 7).

Fig. 5

Cut back jacket pattern and two front pattern pieces from felt. Whipstitch seams together (Fig. 6).

Fig. 7

Sew pom-pom onto back of bunny as if it were poking through back vent of jacket (Fig. 8).

Fig. 8

(Continued)

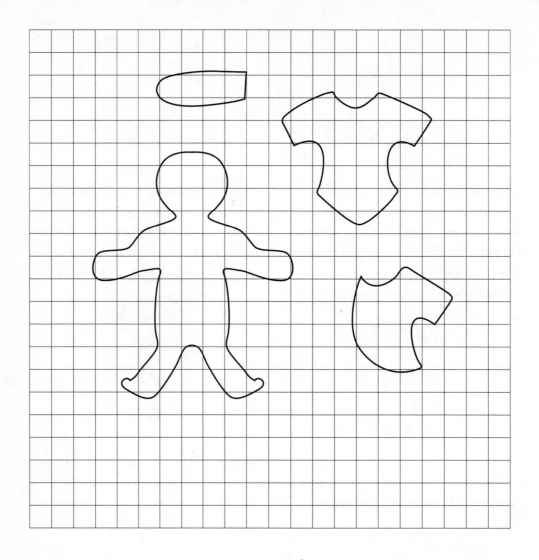

1 square = 1 inch

Bo Peep Puppet
MAKES 1

--- ❖ ---

This makes an adorable Easter morning surprise for children when nestled alongside chocolate eggs and marshmallow chicks in a basket. Sheep puppets have always appealed to kids—remember Lampchop? This one doesn't move its mouth; instead, the fingers are used to work its legs. If you don't own a sewing machine, the puppet can easily be stitched up by hand. Need to bring something to an Easter bazaar? Why not whip up a whole herd of these!

1/4 yard natural color "fleecy" woven wool
scissors
pins
needle
thread (to match wool)
rubber band
sewing machine (optional)
scrap of black felt
cardboard tube from toilet paper roll
cotton or polyester stuffing
fabric glue
black embroidery floss
white shirt buttons
6-inch length of 1/4-inch pink or
blue satin ribbon (optional)

Enlarge pattern to scale. Cut 2 each of body, head, and ear shapes out of wool: cut 2 each of face, head, ear, and hoof shapes out of felt. Cut cardboard tube to 2 1/2 inch length. Pin head and face sections together with fleecy side facing felt. Sew along face seam, 1/4 inch from edge (Fig. 1).

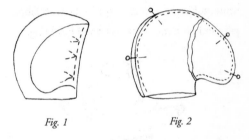

Fig. 1   Fig. 2

(If sewing by hand, trim pieces down by 1/8 inch and whipstitch around all edges of puppet.) Pin entire head sections fleecy sides together and stitch around head 1/4 inch from edge, leaving opening at neck. Clip curves (Fig. 2).

Turn head right side out. Pin hooves along lower leg edges of one body section, against fleecy side, with points facing in (Fig. 3). Baste in place. Pin remaining body section fleecy side down over section with hooves, sandwiching hooves in center. Stitch around sides 1/4 inch from the edge, leaving opening at neck and base. (Fig. 3).

(Continued)

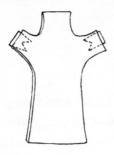

Fig. 3

Tuck head into neck so that neck opening edges align with head facing forward in relationship to the body. Stitch 1/4 inch from edge. Stuff head with some stuffing. Cover cardboard tube with fabric glue and push into neck section of head (Fig. 4).

Fig. 4

Bring neck section of body up around tube. Allow fabric glue to dry with a rubber band around that area (Fig. 5).

Fig. 5

Pin felt ear sections against fleecy side of wool ear sections. Stitch 1/4 inch from edges, leaving opening at base. Turn. Pinch ears together at base, and sew at each side of head. Use black embroidery floss to stitch nostrils (pull through head to both sides.) Sew on button eyes the same way, using embroidery floss. Hem base of puppet with thread (Fig. 6).

Fig. 6

If desired, make bow out of ribbon and tack over one ear with thread.

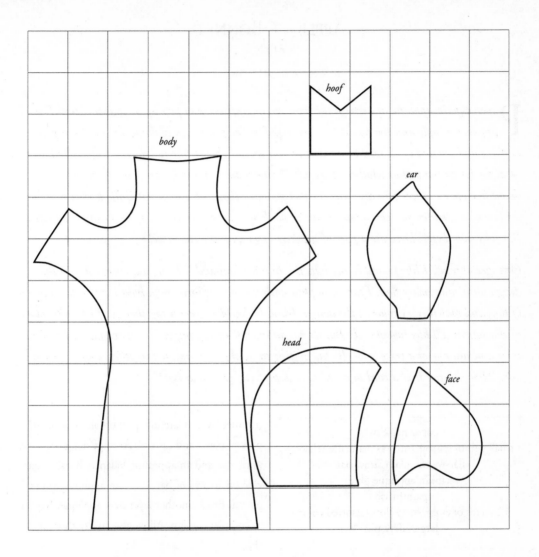

hoof

body

ear

head

face

1 square = 1 inch

APPLIQUÉ BONNET
MAKES 1

❖

*P*aper napkin appliqué is perhaps the most recent craft craze to pop up at country fairs. The process is simple and the results are exciting. The designs, typically floral, are cut from paper napkins and applied to all sorts of surfaces with a special glue (I like to adorn straw hats). They're ideal for Easter bonnets or Mother's Day gifts. Some people hang these on doors or hat racks as decorative pieces; others actually wear them. I'm one of those, because a hat is the perfect sunblock for fair skin. Besides, you can appliqué the same designs on a T-shirt and have a complete outfit. But why stop there? Decorate a pair of sneakers to go with the ensemble!

One special touch I like to add to my hats is a braided hatband. I bring out every color in the design with embroidery floss. I take a napkin with me to the fabric shop, hold it up to the drawers of floss and match every color in the design. I usually braid 12 skeins together, so if I find 6 colors in the pattern, I'll buy two of each. But it's not an exact science; I might buy more of a predominant color and just one of a trace color. It's fascinating to see them all braided together. People always ask, "How did you find a cord to coordinate so perfectly with that hat?"

paper napkins*
small pair of scissors (such as manicure scissors)
flat-weave, plain straw hat
napkin appliqué glue
paintbrush
12 skeins of embroidery floss (assorted colors)
large safety pin

Cut designs from napkins through all plies (this makes them easier to handle). Be sure to cut close enough so that background color is completely trimmed away. Carefully peel off all nonprinted plies of paper and discard. Arrange designs on hat until you find an appealing balance. Brush some glue on an area of hat where an appliqué will be placed. Brush another layer over appliqué. Repeat to complete design. Allow glue to dry thoroughly (Fig. 1).

One by one, unwind each skein of floss, taking care not to tangle it. (This is much easier to do on a long table or the floor.) Lay out the floss, then

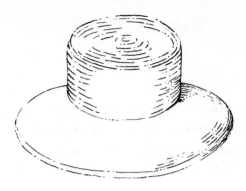

Fig. 1

Fig. 3

double it back, bringing both ends together. Double back again to form a length of 4 strands. Tie a knot at each end to hold strands together. Repeat with each skein, keeping them laid out flat and untangled. Thread skeins onto safety pin through knots at one end. Close safety pin in drawer or cabinet door that will say shut. (You need something that will anchor the pin in place while you braid.) Divide into 3 sections of 4 skeins and braid tightly (Fig. 2).

Fig. 2

When you've finished braiding, tie a tight knot about 3 inches from each end. Trim ends of floss to 1-inch tassels. Tie cord around hat to form a hatband (Fig. 3).

*NOTE: It's worth investing in more expensive napkins that mimic designer chintz, wallpapers, or china patterns. Remember—if a napkin looks too tacky to use at your next party, you certainly wouldn't want to wear it on your head!

HELPFUL HINT: When appliquéing napkins to T-shirts, cover a piece of cardboard with foil and slip it inside the shirt (or shirtsleeve). This will prevent glue from penetrating to the other side of the shirt. Likewise, stuff sneakers with crumpled foil (paper will stick to glue) to hold their shape while working.

May Day Nosegay Wreath
MAKES 1

❖

Wreaths aren't just for Christmas anymore! They've become a year-round door accessory. Nowhere is this more apparent than at a country fair. Strawflower creations in soft pastels are a sure signal of spring. Nosegays of crocheted lace wrapped around tiny bouquets make this wreath special.

5 yards each: $^1/_8$ or $^2/_3$-inch plum and
soft green satin ribbon
12-inch flat twig wreath
six 5-inch crocheted doilies
scissors
fabric glue
hot glue gun
assorted dried strawflowers
dried baby's breath
floral wire

Cut six 9-inch pieces from each color of ribbon (these will be used on nosegays). Hold remaining long ribbons together and thread in and out of twigs around wreath. Tie ends together in bow. Trim long streamers, fold into extra loops, and tie into bow (Fig. 1).

Fig. 1

Cut doilies in half into semicircles. Roll each piece into cone, holding the third that overlaps between your thumb and finger. Spread glue on adjoining surfaces of overlapping edges, and pinch together for several minutes until cone is secure. Allow to

Opposite: Appliqué Bonnet, page 16

dry. Thread 6-inch ribbon around upper edge of each cone and tie in tiny bow on front of cone, trimming streamers to adjust to bows (Fig. 2).

Fig. 2

Trim stems of strawflowers and baby's breath so flowers fit into cones. Divide into twelve attractive arrangements. Bind stems of the tiny bouquets with small pieces of floral wire. Use hot glue gun to secure bouquets into cones, forming nosegays (Fig. 3).

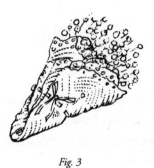

Fig. 3

Arrange nosegays around wreath to your satisfaction, then anchor in place with hot glue (Fig. 4). Make loop of floral wire and twist into back of wreath for hanging.

Fig. 4

Opposite: Scissors Doll in Sponge-Painted Sewing Kit, page 20

Scissors Doll in Sponge-Painted Sewing Kit
MAKES 1

❖

The "scissors' keeper" doll has long been a tradition among country quilters, and it actually served a practical purpose. Anyone who sews will tell you that it's frustrating to misplace scissors. With scraps of fabric all around, this happens quite frequently. No wonder the keeper is such a popular item at country fairs. It comes in a sewing box painted like classic sponged pottery, and makes a wonderful Mother's Day gift.

2¹/₂-inch clothespin
black and red acrylic paint
small paintbrush
1¹/₈ yards ¹/₄-inch blue satin ribbon
small embroidery scissors
hot glue gun or thick craft glue
scissors
needle
thread
5-inch circle of blue homespun fabric
cotton or polyester stuffing
scrap of ecru lace
3 small buttons
SPONGE-PAINTED SEWING KIT
(instructions follow)

Fig. 1

Paint hair on top of clothespin, and two dots for eyes, with black paint. Paint a tiny mouth with red paint (Fig. 1).

Allow to dry. Fold ribbon in half and loop through one ring of scissors' handle. Use hot glue to attach free ends of ribbon to back of clothespin (Fig. 2).

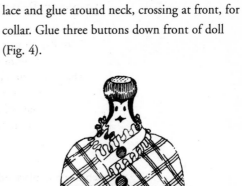

Fill circle with stuffing and insert clothespin in center. Apply glue around "neck" and pull gathers tightly up around glue. Cut 2-inch strip of lace and glue around neck, crossing at front, for collar. Glue three buttons down front of doll (Fig. 4).

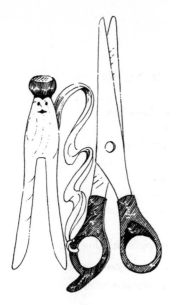

Fig. 2

Baste a gathering stitch around edges of fabric circle (Fig. 3).

Fig. 4

(Continued)

Fig. 3

SPONGE-PAINTED SEWING KIT

7- or 8-inch wooden Brie cheese box
aluminum foil
white (or ecru) and blue acrylic paint
paintbrush
natural sea sponge
aluminum pie pan

Open box and place lid and base open side down on aluminum foil. Brush white or ecru paint onto box. Allow to dry. Apply second coat and let dry thoroughly. If necessary, tear edges of sponge to make more ragged. Pour blue paint into pie tin and blot sponge in paint. Print irregular splashes of paint all over top and bottom of box. When dry, remove from foil.

Raggedy Wrapped Rope Basket
makes one 9-inch basket

❖

*T*he old art of wrapping rags around ropes around bowls to make baskets has never been easier. Since the invention of hot glue guns, this one-time needle and thread project takes no time at all. What a perfect Mother's Day craft for any spring fair!

21-inch length of 45-inch cotton calico
ruler
scissors
pencil
glue gun (use *hot* melt gun and glue sticks)
6 yards of 1/2-inch cotton cording
31/4-inch high, 8-inch diameter mixing bowl
aluminum foil
large heavy can (for a weight)

At the selvage of fabric, mark 11/2-inch intervals with a pencil. Clip marks with scissors and tear into 45-inch long strips. Trim away any loose threads. Begin with the right side of a fabric strip facing you and perpendicular to the end of cording. Secure fabric to cording with a small bead of glue. Wrapt strip around cord, using an under-and-over technique, overlapping fabric by about 1/2 inch. At the end of the strip, secure with a small bead of hot glue. Glue the end of the next strip over the end of the previous strip, overlapping by 1/4 inch. Continue to wrap and add strips until cord is completely covered.

Begin coiling base on a flat surface covered with foil. Fold end of cord over by 1 inch and secure with hot glue. Begin coiling cord around end, securing at intervals with hot glue (Fig. 1). Once you've reached the diameter of the bowl's base, place bowl on top (anchor bowl by placing heavy can in the center). Continue to coil and glue cord around bowl, turning as you work. When you reach the rim of the bowl, cut cord at an angle and glue in place, cut side down. Remove can from the center of basket (Fig. 2).

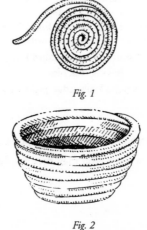

Fig. 1

Fig. 2

Bow Pillow
MAKES 1

❖

*T*hese are by far the simplest pillows you could ever make. The covers require no zippers and can easily be removed for washing. When making them for myself or friends, I choose fabrics that will work with a familiar decor. However, at a crafts fair or bazaar you're dealing with the interiors of unknown homes. One way around this dilemma is to research the season's latest home catalogs. If you cut the pillows from some of the most popular designer bed sheets, people just "have to have them" to complete their set. These directions are based on one pillow, but you can generally get more mileage out of a continuous length of fabric (or bed sheet) when making multiple pillows; there's less waste in the cutting. It's always tempting to ignore the fabric grain when laying out patterns. Don't fall into that trap. It's important that these pillows be cut on the bias.

---

yardstick
roll of wide paper
pencil
pins
scissors
1³/8 yards 54-inch fabric
(or use a bed sheet)
1¹/2 yards ¹/2-inch double-fold bias tape
(choose a color coordinating with pattern)
thread (to match fabric)
sewing machine
16-inch square knife-edge pillow form

Enlarge pattern on large sheet of paper according to dimensions given (you may need to piece paper together with tape). Cut out pattern and lay on bias of fabric (Fig. 1).

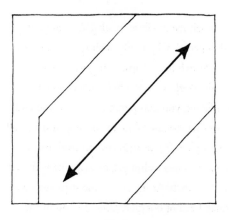

Fig. 1

Pin pattern to fabric and cut out. Bind each angled end with bias tape, folding at point and turning under at edges (Fig. 2).

Turn case right side out. Slip pillow inside, positioning it in center. Bring ends up and tie in knot (Fig. 4).

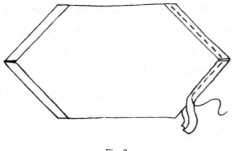

Fig. 2

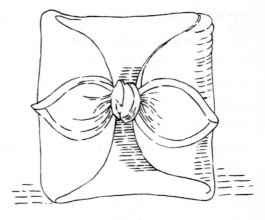

Fig. 4

Fold fabric in half, right sides together. Stitch unbound edge (Fig 3). Press seam flat.

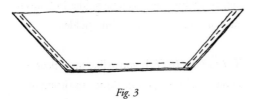

Fig. 3

HOSPITALITY LUMINARY
MAKES 1

❖

The pineapple has been a symbol of hospitality since colonial times. From doormats to flatware, the motif now welcomes people throughout today's homes. I've always been intrigued by luminaries; lanternlike vessels for candles that glow through tiny holes. They're really quite simple to make, using the traditional tin punch technique with a paint can, hammer, and nail. When working on flat sheets of metal, a board is placed underneath for support. However, this isn't possible when working on curved surfaces. Solution: Fill the paint can with water and freeze it! The ice provides a hard surface to absorb the nail punches and preserves the shape of the can.

---

tracing paper
wax crayon
masking tape
hammer and nail
1 quart paint can with or without handles (label removed)*
gloves (optional)
epoxy glue
votive candle holder and candle

Photocopy and enlarge pattern. Fill can with water to within 1 inch of top. Freeze until solid, at least 24 hours (do not place lid on can while freezing). Remove can from freezer. (If can is too cold to handle comfortably, wear gloves.) Use nail or a hole punch to poke holes in the pattern. Tape pattern to can and mark through holes with crayon. Reposition pattern on opposite side of can and repeat. Use hammer and nail to punch through holes along lines about 1/8 inch apart. Allow ice to melt, and drain can. Clean off any remaining crayon marks. Dry can thoroughly. Use epoxy to anchor votive candle holder in bottom center of can. Insert candle into holder.

HELPFUL HINT: If you're like most people, you don't have the perfect paint can sitting on the garage shelf. Chances are it has several years on it, along with layers of dried paint drips, so I always buy a fresh new can for making a luminary. Admittedly, I'm not always in the midst of a painting project. Solution: Buy a can of basic white primer. No one can ever have enough. You'll need it for some future paint job, regardless of color. I transfer the primer into a plastic tub with a tightly fitting lid, and clean out the can before the primer has a chance to dry.

Opposite: Hospitality Luminary, page 26

Fig. 1 (Pattern is to scale)

Fig. 2

Opposite: Turtles in a Nutshell, page 33

Crazy Caterpillar
MAKES ONE 44-INCH CATERPILLAR

❖

This whimsical stuffed toy is as much fun for adults as it is for children. Using Victorian-type fabrics such as brocades, damasks, and printed velvets makes them look very eclectic. Once you get started, it's easy to sew up several at the same time.

tailor's chalk
yardstick
1/4 yard "dressy-looking" fabric such as brocade, damask, upholstery silk, or velvet (should be at least 45 inches wide)
2 1/4 yards of drapery fringe
scissors
pins
needle
sewing machine
thread (to match fabric)
1/2-inch plastic-coated electrical wire
polyester stuffing
2 antique-looking buttons with dark stone in center

Split fabric in half, lengthwise so that you have two 4 1/2-inch × 45-inch strips. Place strips on top of each other and trim one end so that the edges are rounded (head). Trim opposite end to a point (tail) (Fig. 1).

Fig. 1

Cut fringe in half. Each strip will be 1 1/8 yards. Starting on each side (from the top of the tail) pin fringe to the right side of one fabric piece. Fringe should be facing inward and stop about 4 1/2 inches on each side from the end of the head. Baste fringe in place (Fig. 2).

Fig. 2

Pin remaining section of fabric, right-side down, against fabric. Sew around fabric, 1/2 inch from edge, leaving five 2-inch openings as shown (Fig. 3). (Openings are necessary for turning and stuffing caterpillar.)

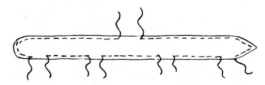

Fig. 3

Turn fabric right-side out through center side opening, and press (Fig. 4).

Fig. 4

Slip wire through opening at head and gently push it through to the tip of the tail. Use openings to stuff caterpillar, making sure that the wire is encased by the stuffing and running through the center of the figure. Slipstitch openings. Sew buttons about 3 inches from end of head for "eyes." Use multi-strand shank of thread to connect buttons behind fabric. Bend caterpiller into desired position (Fig. 5).

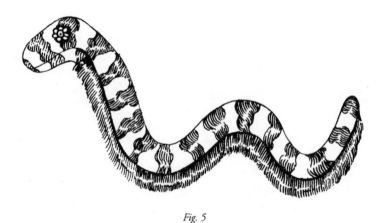

Fig. 5

SUMMER

❖

Summer is a time of travel. No matter where you live, you will most likely be going somewhere else. Since state and country fairs are a major tourist attraction, this is when small towns start pitching big pink and white tents. It's carnival time in the country! Ferris wheels start arriving at the fairgrounds. Sounds of merry-go-round melodies enchant the summer nights. Cotton candy abounds, and everybody has a good time. Now is the season to stock up on crafts you can only find in summer: that tote bag to take to the beach, the perfect director's chairs for your deck, or seashell lamps for a candlelight dinner by the shore. Other collectibles are child oriented and whimsical in nature, such as garden toads, turtles in a nutshell, or Indian crab claw dolls.

The crafts of these summer fairs are often meant to be souvenirs of a special day and place. After all, don't we wish our vacations would last forever? When travelers return home with their treasures, they have year-round memories of summertime magic.

SUMMER

❖

Turtles in a Nutshell

Indian Crab Claw Dolls

Garden Toads and Toadstools

Mailbox Barn

Mantel Mallard

Country Cow Door Bells

Three Little Pigs Pin or Barrette

Crew-Cut Coconuts

Postage Stamp Lapel Pins

Block Print Baby Bib

Betsy Ross Beach Bag

Sunshine Director's Chairs

Seaside Candlesticks

Turtles in a Nutshell

❖

Here's another entertaining craft for kids that brings me back to my childhood. We were always on the lookout for a new box turtle to add to our collection. When my brother or I spotted one crossing the road, we'd shout at Dad to stop the car. He'd always pull over, pick it up, and put it in the trunk. I now feel a little sorry for some of those pet turtles. They usually stayed on the back porch, where they'd climb up the screens and fall on their backs. Other popular places where neighborhood kids kept turtles included basement window wells. However, this was a problem when a sudden thunderstorm dropped a foot of rain overnight! And then there was the Saturday afternoon turtle derby, when all the kids brought their "fastest" turtle to a designated driveway. Names like Speedy, Peppy, and Groford (my turtle) were painted on their shells. Inevitably, half the turtles "ran" in the opposite direction from the finish line. Groford hardly budged but usually won the race by default.

Poor Groford suffered the indignities of suburban childhood. Perhaps he'd have been better off if we'd left him on that country road. (Then again, he could have been run over by a truck.) As an adult, I now advise children to leave wild creatures in the wild, but kids will always have a natural attraction to turtles. These walnut-shell versions work well as refrigerator magnets (and they don't fall off the fridge while they're climbing it!).

(Continued)

scraps of calico in turtle colors
(greens or browns)
pins
needle
thread (to match calico)
cotton or polyester stuffing
black embroidery floss
walnuts
nutcracker and nut pick
refrigerator magnets
thick craft glue

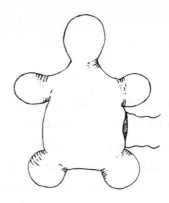

Fig. 2

Use pattern to cut turtles from calico scraps. You'll need two pieces of the same fabric for each turtle. Pin pieces right sides together. Whipstitch around edges, leaving an opening at the side to turn (Fig. 1). Turn turtles right side out and stuff. Be sure to push stuffing

(Stitch mouth along seam at end of head.) Crack walnuts in half, taking care not to damage shells by opening them along the natural seam. Pick nutmeats out of shell. Glue magnets to underside of turtles, and walnut shells on top (Fig. 3). Try not to let glue ooze out from under shell.

Fig. 3

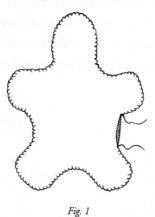

Fig. 1

firmly into head and legs (Fig. 2). Slipstitch side opening. Use black embroidery floss to make eyes and mouth.

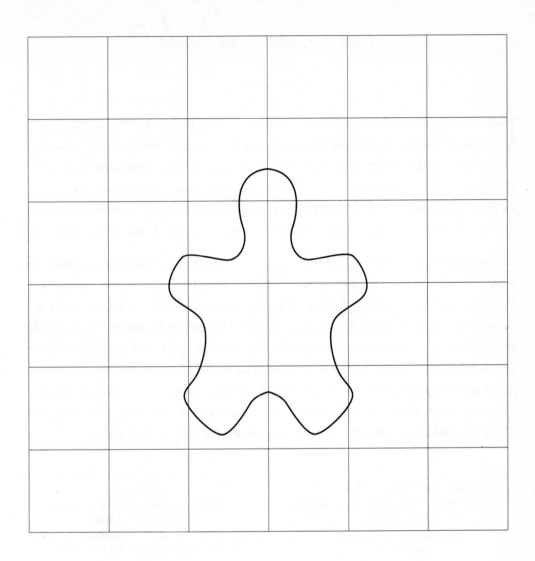

1 square = 1 inch

INDIAN CRAB CLAW DOLLS
MAKES 1

— ❖ —

I remember the first time I saw a crab claw doll. It was at an Indian craft shop during one of our family vacations. I must have been about seven years old and I thought it was the most fascinating thing I'd ever seen. After much begging and pleading, my parents bought it for me. (My brother wanted a tomahawk . . . so he could scalp me!) The doll was broken by the time we got home. I think my brother clubbed it with his souvenir. He was inspired by a dinner we had had at a Maryland crab house; everyone at the restaurant was beating boiled crabs with hammers.

After my doll's demise, I was determined to recreate it. However, my first attempt developed a very unpleasant odor . . . much like a really dead fish! It's not enough to simply save the crab claws from dinner. I later learned that they first have to be soaked in a bleach solution, then dried in the sun. I love making these for bazaars and craft fairs. Once you get started, you can practically mass-produce them. I even enjoy collecting the crab claws, since I get to cook a lot of crab dinners. The secret is not to crack the claw shell; the meat should be pulled through the leg joint with a pick. I warn everyone at the table: "If you smash a crab claw, you won't get any dessert!" Crab claws vary in size, which makes the dolls even more interesting. Maryland crab claws range from $2^{1}/2$ to $3^{1}/2$ inches in length, while Alaskan King crab claws can be up to 6 inches.

crab claws (with first leg joint)	toothpicks
$^{1}/2$ cup bleach mixed with 1 quart water	seed beads (assorted colors such as turquoise and red)
aluminum foil	tree limb, 2 inches to 4 inches in diameter (size in proportion to crab claws)
ecru and tan acrylic paint	
paintbrush	ruler
fine point black and red permanent ink felt-tip markers	pencil
thick craft glue and epoxy glue or super bonding glue	cross cut saw
	sandpaper
craft feathers (both natural and dyed)	file, if needed

Carefully examine crab claws to be certain that all meat has been removed. If not, remove with seafood pick. Soak claws in bleach solution for 12 hours or overnight. Rinse several times to remove bleach. Spread claws out on tray and dry thoroughly in the sun (this could take a couple of days). Cover work surface with aluminum foil so painted claws are less likely to stick. Paint claws one side at a time, allowing each side to dry before turning over. When painting clothes on the claw, think of the leg joint as the head, and the base of the claw as the neck. Do not color these parts, but paint ecru from the neck down. Paint tips of claws tan, for moccasins. When both sides have been painted and dried, add details with black marking pen. Outline neck opening of shirt, and tops of moccasins. Draw lines for where arms are folded into sleeves. Draw eyes and nose. With red pen, draw mouth (Fig. 1).

Fig. 1

Use thick craft glue to glue one natural feather, and one or two colored feathers, into opening in top of head (leg joint, Fig. 2). With toothpicks, apply epoxy to seed beads and decorate shirt neck, buttons, and sides of pants. Allow to dry.

Fig. 2

Mark limb in 3/4-inch sections with pencil. Cut with saw and sand cut edges, leaving bark around sides. (You'll need to make as many bases as you have crab claws.) Dab epoxy on bottom of moccasins and glue doll upright on base, propping doll up while drying (Fig. 3). If claws are too pointed to stand upright, you may have to file tips down before painting.

Fig. 3

NOTE: If you find gluing beads frustrating or tedious, try using tubes of dimensional paints instead. When piped through the nozzle, little droplets dry to look like raised beads.

Garden Toads and Toadstools
Makes 1 Toad and 2 Toadstools

❖

*T*his *is a great project for children to make or simply appreciate. Though nothing more than painted pebbles, these "toads" and "toadstools" transform the average flower bed into an enchanted garden. Kids love to hide them all around a backyard vegetable patch—they make weeding more fun. Nurturing an interest in gardening helps create a respect for nature and where food comes from. It also creates enthusiasm to "eat stuff that's good for you"!*

Smooth, flat round and oval stones*
small round pebbles
epoxy, glue, or super bonding glue**
aluminum foil
acrylic paint: 2 shades of olive green or
khaki brown (for toads,
one shade should be the darker
value of the other),
white, black, and assorted colors
(for toadstools)
paintbrushes
matte acrylic polymer

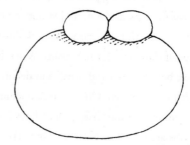

Fig. 1

For toads you'll want to select stones that are slightly oval and 3 to 4 inches in diameter. For toadstools, use flat round stones. The base should always be smaller than the cap. When making toads, glue two pebbles on top for eyes (Fig. 1). Glue caps of toadstools onto stems (Fig. 2). Allow to dry. Place stones to be painted on foil so they don't stick. Paint toads with base coat of either olive or khaki in lighter shade.

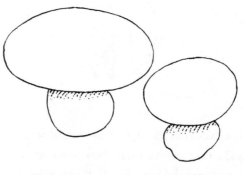

Fig. 2

Allow to dry. Use fine brush and the darker shade of paint to add features, (Fig. 3) including legs, spots on back, mouth, and outlines of eyes. Paint eyes white. Allow to dry and add pupils with black paint (Fig. 3).

Fig. 4

Fig. 3

Toadstools can be almost any whimsical color. Be sure to paint stem and underside of cap the same color. Paint top of cap a contrasting shade. Allow to dry. Paint spots on cap the same color as used for stem (Fig. 4). Coat toads and toadstools with polymer to seal paint.

NOTE: Check your local garden or landscaping center for river rocks and beach pebbles. This is really the best source for stones that are smooth and fairly uniform in size and shape.

**NOTE:* When using epoxy or super bonding glues, it's always best for an adult to actually bond the stones. These adhesives should not be handled by children. Once the stones are set, the toads and toadstools make a great painting project for kids.

MAILBOX BARN
MAKES 1

❖

*C*ruising down the country roads of Connecticut, you can't see the houses for the trees. After a while you begin to recognize which rural route mailbox belongs to which drive. Lately I've noticed a trend toward quirky customized versions of those classic steel boxes with red flags. On one trip I spotted Dalmatians, dachshunds, pigs, and cows posted alongside the road. I wondered where they were coming from, and my answer came when I arrived at my destination, a country crafts fair. Here I found all sorts of amusing mailboxes for sale. They were more than receptacles for bills; these were statements of self-expression! One resembled a deer about to dart across the street. Rather than cause any traffic accidents, I opted for a charming, low-key barn. It's really the most logical conversion—after all, dairy barns look sort of like great big mailboxes sitting in a field. This one's also easy to make. All you need is paint (no legs or antlers!).

traditional domed mailbox
aluminum foil
barn red spray paint (for metal)
masking tape
ruler
pencil
assorted paintbrushes
acrylic paint: slate gray, black,
white, green, yellow
matte spray acrylic sealer

Place mailbox on aluminum foil and spray red. Use enough coats to give opaque coverage, allowing paint to dry between coats. Use white paint for windows and doors, according to scale. For example, if your mailbox is about 18 inches × 8 inches × 6 inches, paint four 4-inch × 4-inch doors (one at each end and centered on sides). Paint four 3-inch × 2 1/2-inch windows, on each side of side doors (Fig. 1).

When dry, mask off roofline about 5 inches from base (1 inch above doors); paint gray. When dry, paint thin lines of black horizontally across roof at 1/4-inch intervals. Paint irregular marks between lines for shingles. Use thin brush to paint wisps of grass around base of mailbox. Paint a few yellow dots for dandelions (Fig. 2).

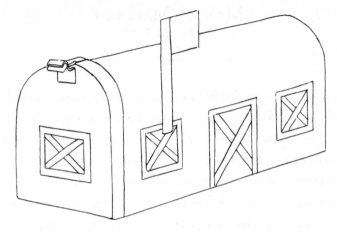

Fig. 1

Fig. 2

Mantel Mallard
makes 1

❖

Duck decoys perched over the fireplace are a classic country accent. Many of these hand-carved sculptures are true works of art. There used to be a shop in Essex, Connecticut, devoted to decoys. I loved browsing through the collection, and marveled at the distinctive details and expression of every bird. No two ducks were exactly alike, just as there are subtle differences in every living creature. I admit there are times when all ducks really do seem to come from the same mold (especially when a whole flock decides to cross a rural road). However, having raised several Easter pets, I learned to appreciate individual personalities. It's that personality that master craftsmen are able to capture in their carvings. Perhaps it's the duck's, but more likely it's the artist's. Needless to say, the work of such artists is sought by collectors and commands a steep price. I wouldn't attempt to tell you how to carve a decoy in this book. (Frankly, I get intimidated whittling soap.) Still, you can stuff a handsome specimen and never have to shoot it! This fabric decoy is stitched up and stiffened with gesso before painting. You can sew a whole flock to sell at a fair, or make one special family heirloom for your fireplace mantel.

1/2 yard cotton muslin	buttonhole twist
paper	2 1/2-inch animal eyes with shank
pencil	1-inch flat paintbrush
scissors	gesso
pins	fine sandpaper
needle	acrylic paints: off-white, yellow ochre, teal green, brown, slate gray, black
sewing machine	
thread (to match muslin)	aluminum pie pans
cotton or polyester stuffing	natural sponge
dollmaking needle	assorted small paintbrushes

Opposite: *Indian Crab Claw Dolls, page 36*

Enlarge patterns to scale, transferring pieces onto sheets of paper. Pin pattern pieces to muslin, cutting two pieces for body and one piece each for base, tail, and upper and lower bill. Right sides together, pin body pieces together and stitch 1/4 inch from edges, leaving base, tail, and bill openings (Fig. 1). Stitch dart in lower bill. Pin upper bill to lower bill right sides together. Stitch 1/4 inch from edges and clip curves (Fig. 2). Pin

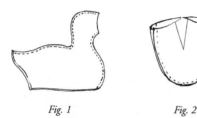

Fig. 1   Fig. 2

bill to body right sides together, aligning dart with neck seam. Stitch 1/4 inch from edges of neck and bill (Fig. 3). Pin tail to back of body and stitch 1/4

Fig. 3

inch from edge. Clip curves. Pin bottom to base of body and tail panels. Sew 1/4 inch from edge, allowing 3-inch opening to turn duck. Clip curves (Fig. 4). Turn body right side out and stuff.

Fig. 4

Slipstitch opening (Fig. 5). Use dollmaking needle and button hole twist to sew on eyes. Connect eyes through center of head, pulling tightly to indent slightly. Wet 1-inch brush with water and

Fig. 5

dip in gesso. Paint duck with gesso, saturating fabric. Allow to dry thoroughly. Sand lightly. Repeat with 2 or 3 coats of gesso, sanding after each coat dries. Pour some gray paint into an aluminum pie pan and dip moist natural sponge in paint. Sponge-paint duck body gray; allow to dry. Use brush to paint bill ochre, and head teal green. Sponge brown paint at breast feathers, wingtips, and base of tail. When dry, paint white ring around mallard's neck. Accent tips of feathers with white and black paint, using brushes. Allow to dry (Fig. 6).

Fig. 6

(Continued)

Opposite: Garden Toads and Toadstools, page 38

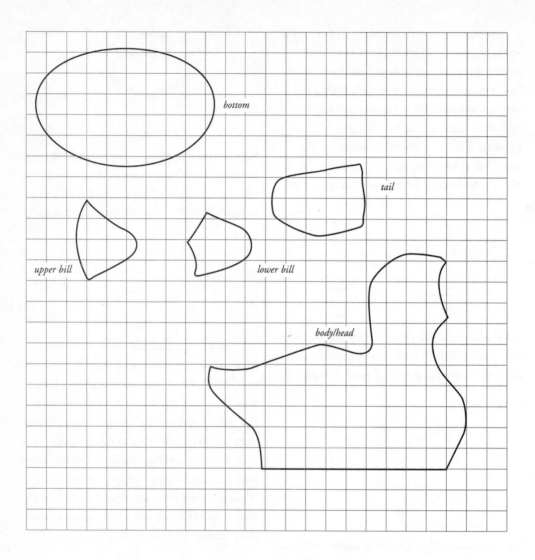

bottom

tail

upper bill

lower bill

body/head

1 square = 1 inch

COUNTRY COW DOOR BELLS
MAKES 1 PAIR

❖

*B*lack and white bovines, grazing in bucolic settings, have captured the hearts of America. All of a sudden cows are everywhere, from ceramic cream pitchers to life-size stuffed lawn toys. They used to be seen at country fairs, weighing in for the grand prize. Now they're the most popular motif for all sorts of handcrafts. These cow bells are painted with that characteristic piebald pattern of black and white Holsteins. They make attractive doorknob ornaments to announce the arrival of family and friends.

2 full-size cow bells
aluminum foil
black and white acrylic paint
matte acrylic polymer
paintbrush
1 yard $^3/_4$-inch red and white
checked ribbon

Fig. 1

Place bells open end down on aluminum foil. Paint with two coats of white paint, allowing to dry between coats (it's important that coverage be completely opaque). When applying black patches to bell, try visualizing a country cow for your model (Fig. 1). If necessary, give second coat of paint to black patches for thorough coverage. When dry, apply a coat of acrylic polymer as sealer. When sealer is dry, cut ribbon in half and string through loop of each bell. Knot ends of ribbon (Fig. 2).

Fig. 2

THREE LITTLE PIGS PIN OR BARRETTE
MAKES 1

❖

*C*hildren delight in miniature stuffed animal pins—and so do adults. One of these pins on a
lady's lapel becomes a novel fashion accessory that's bound to start a conversation. These are
so small that they really must be sewn by hand. The secret to working with felt is whipstitching
close to the edge (there's practically no seam), and using a manicurist's orange stick to help turn
and stuff the fabric. Three little pigs in a row can also be glued to the back of a barrette.

scraps of peach or pink felt
needle and thread
orange stick
cotton or polyester stuffing
black embroidery floss
sew-on pin clasps or barrette
hot glue (for barrette)

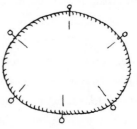

Fig. 2

Use pattern to cut 6 felt ovals for head, 6 circles
for snout, and 6 ears. Pinch ears in half and
stitch at base (Fig. 1). Stitch to outer edges of

Fig. 1

felt circle, facing inward (Fig. 2). Place another
circle on top and whipstitch around edges, leaving

space to turn fabric (Fig. 3). Turn fabric through
hole, using orange stick if necessary to push it
through. Fill with stuffing just until lightly

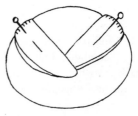

Fig. 3

padded. Slipstitch opening (Fig. 4). Place two
circles together for snout. Whipstitch around

Fig. 4

edges, leaving small opening to turn fabric (you'll need the stick). Slipstitch opening. Place snout on face and anchor in place by sewing nostrils with black embroidery floss: sew two

dots on small felt circle, pulling floss completely through back of head. Sew on 2 dots for eyes (Fig. 5). Sew pins to backs of felt heads. If

Fig. 5

making barrette, line heads up side by side across band and attach with hot glue (Fig. 6).

Fig. 6

(Continued)

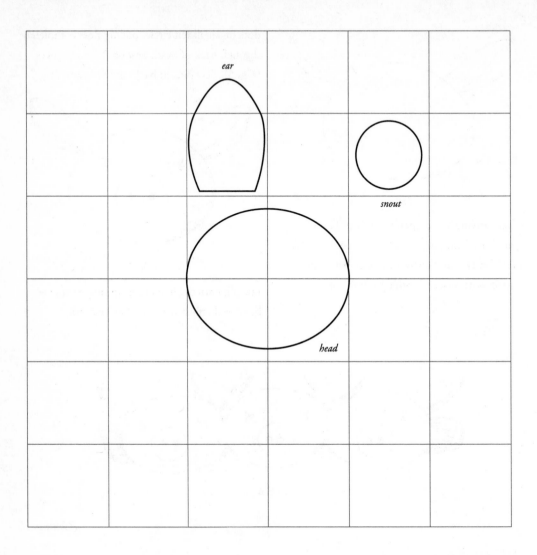

1 square = 1 inch

CREW-CUT COCONUTS
MAKES 2

❖

These amusing fellows look like cartoon characters. Kids love to watch the grass grow from the tops of their heads. They will need weekly hair cuts or their "flat tops" will soon turn into Rapunzel's long locks!

---

2 mature coconuts
cross cut saw
vise
sharp stiff knife
drill with 1/2-inch bit
2 walnut shell halves
6 Brazil nuts
four 1/2-inch to 3/4-inch glue-on hobby eyes
hot melt glue gun
potting soil
grass seed

---

on a Brazil nut (crescent shape facing up in a "smile") for a mouth and one on each side for ears. Glue on hobby eyes. Fill coconuts with potting soil and moisten with water. Cover soil with a thick layer of grass seed and keep moist at all times. Grass should start growing in 5 days to 2 weeks, depending upon the variety used.

Anchor each coconut in a vise and saw off upper one-third. Drain out liquid and score white meat with a knife in cube-like sections. Pry meat out of shell with knife or other tool, taking care not to damage shell. Drill a small hole in the bottom of each shell (for water drainage). Glue a walnut shell (cut side down) in the center of each coconut for a nose. Glue

POSTAGE STAMP LAPEL PINS
MAKES 1

❖

*W*hether it's Elvis or an endangered species, people have a passion for postage stamps. Stamp collecting has been called "the hobby of kings and the king of hobbies"—reputed *philatelists* include King George V of England and Franklin D. Roosevelt. The U.S. Postal Service regards its limited edition stamps as the one lucrative aspect of its business, and markets them aggressively. Stamps are historic records, which makes even the most contemporary ones modern collectibles. And when it comes to collectors of all kinds, you'll find them at country fairs.

Converting stamps into jewelry occurred to me by sheer happenstance one day. Returning from the post office, I had a book of wild duck stamps sticking out from the breast pocket of my blazer. I caught a glimpse of it in the mirror and thought, Why not turn these into lapel pins? I later mounted some for a bazaar, where they were an instant hit.

1/8-inch thick basswood squares or rectangles, cut 1/2-inch larger than stamps
fine sandpaper
aluminum foil
spray paint: gold, brass, silver, black or color to complement stamp
matte acrylic polymer
paintbrush
collector's postage stamps
glue-on pin clasps
epoxy or super bonding glue

Sand pieces of wood until surface and edges are smooth. Arrange on foil and coat lightly with spray paint. Allow to dry. Turn over and spray underside. Apply one more coat of paint to each side, taking care not to spray too heavily, or paint will puddle. Dry thoroughly between coats. When wood is dry, brush lightly with coat of polymer. Center stamp so that wood frames it evenly around edges. Allow to set. Apply top coat of polymer and dry thoroughly. Turn pieces over and apply polymer to back, allowing to dry. Glue pins on back with epoxy or super bonding glue.

Opposite: Postage Stamp Lapel Pins, page 50

HELPFUL HINT: I think canceled stamps have more character, especially when worn as a fashion accessory. Those lines give a stamp its own sense of history. Where did it come from? Who was it sent to? Maybe it's a romantic whim, but I like to think every stamp has a story. It's simple to steam stamps off old envelopes with a teakettle. Recycling old stamps makes sense if you're making these for a crafts fair. Think of all the money you'll save on postage!

Opposite: Block Print Baby Bib, page 52

BLOCK PRINT BABY BIB
MAKES 1

❖

*B*aby *clothes and crafts are always well represented at country fairs. Where else can people seek out one-of-a-kind handmade garments and gifts for that special infant. Popular items range from heirloom-quality christening gowns and crocheted booties to novelty bonnets and baby shirts. For practical purposes, I've chosen not to focus on intricate needlework projects in this book. That's what I like about block print baby bibs: even if you can't sew a stitch, you can still print with those classic wooden blocks. The letters make ideal paint stamps and come out looking just like the blocks themselves only backward! If you're making a bib for a specific child, you can use the blocks to print his or her name. No time to sew? No talent for sewing? No problem. Just print on store-bought bibs.*

large sheet of paper
yardstick
pencil
scissors
pins
1/2 yard gingham or homespun (choose a primary color similar to a block)
1/2 yard opaque white cotton or natural muslin (use muslin if using homespun)
wooden baby blocks
aluminum pie pans
fabric paints in colors to match blocks
paper towels
piping to match gingham or homespun
button to match piping
sewing machine needle
thread (to match cotton or muslin)

Enlarge pattern to scale on paper and cut one piece from gingham and one piece from cotton. Select block you want to use for printing on the cotton or muslin. You can print the blocks in a random pattern, print a child's name, or simply print BABY, though you will need to hold the block upside down for B to get it to print correctly. (You can also print random alphabet letters around a word.) Of course, because some letters will print backwards, you may just want to use picture blocks. For every color of block you use, you'll need a pie pan and the corresponding color of paint. Squeeze a small amount of paint into each pan, forming a very shallow puddle. Practice printing on paper towels. Do you like the effect of the first print? Or do you prefer blotting the paint on a towel and going with the second or third print? This is what you need to work out before you print on fabric (much depends on your brand of paint and technique). Once you've decided on a design, print on cotton or muslin bib piece and follow manufacturer's directions for setting paint (if necessary).

After paint has dried and been set, pin piping around edges and neck hole; piping should be facing inward, with stitching line 1/2 inch from edge. Baste piping in place (Fig. 1). Pin fabric

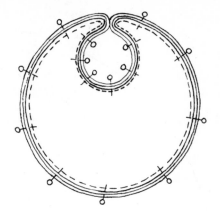

Fig. 2

Fig. 1

Fig. 3

face down on gingham, right sides together. Stitch around fabric just inside line of basting stitches allowing a 3-inch opening at side to turn (Fig. 2). Turn fabric and press. Topstitch around edge of bib 1/8 inch from piping. Make buttonhole at one side of neck opening and sew button at other side (Fig. 3).

HELPFUL HINT: Baby stains are hard on fabrics. Super strength stain removers may remove some of the fabric paint as well. I always give bibs a coating of spray fabric protector.

(Continued)

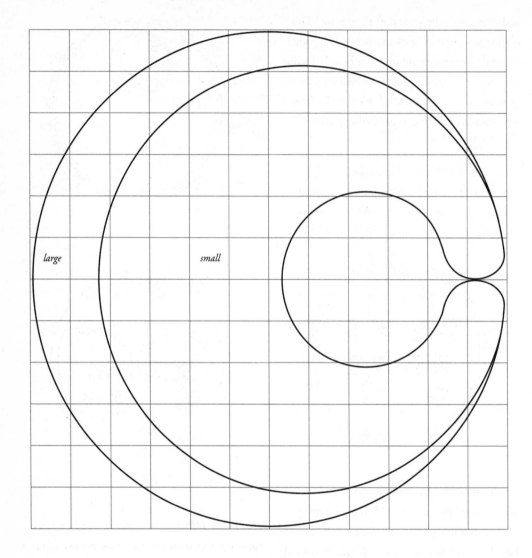

large

small

1 square = 1 inch

BETSY ROSS BEACH BAG
MAKES 1

❖

Whether you're in pursuit of the perfect tan or simply on a summer picnic, everyone can use one of these patriotic totes. I personally take three along to all my seaside outings—one for goopy, gloppy mosquito lotions and sunscreens, one for sandy stuff, and one for food (mixing any of these together is a very unpleasant combination). The bags are also the right size for carting some bottles of wine, water, or soda to a Fourth of July barbecue. There's one every year in my neighborhood. We gather along the seawall under the stars to watch the fireworks across the harbor. It's my favorite night of the year, and each year brings me back to every year past. Some of my flag bags date back to those early memories. They started out as dark blue denim, but like a faded pair of jeans—or Old Glory—they just get better with age. Similar totes often show up at midsummer country fairs in various patterns of red, white, and blue. My version incorporates the 13 stripes and a circle of stars, just the way Betsy Ross would have done it!

tailor's chalk
yardstick
1/2 yard white cotton broadcloth
1/2 yard red cotton broadcloth
1 yard 45-inch dark blue denim
scissors
pins
needle
sewing machine
thread (to match blue denim and white cotton)
13 white star-shaped buttons

Use chalk and yardstick to mark sections of fabric before cutting. Cut twelve 2-inch × 19-inch strips from white cotton. Cut thirteen 2-inch × 19-inch strips from red cotton. Cut denim into 3 rectangles: 8 inches × 9 inches for blue flag field, 14 inches × 19 inches for plain side of tote and 14 inches × 37 inches for lining of tote. Cut two 5-inch × 18-inch strips of denim for handles. Sew red and white strips side by side lengthwise, beginning and ending with a red strip; allow 1/2-inch seams so stripes will be 1 inch wide. Press seams open. Arrange striped section right side up on flat surface (Fig. 1). With wrong side up, fold in 1/2 inch along two adjacent sides of the 8-inch × 9-inch blue denim rectangle and press, mitering corner (Fig. 2). Place blue field in upper left corner of flag, with raw edges matching edges of striped flag and pressed edges

(Continued)

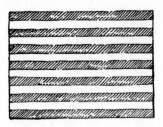

Fig. 1

facing down (Fig. 3). Pin in place and topstitch.
Sew stars in circle on blue field (Fig. 3). Pin

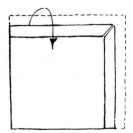

Fig. 2

14-inch × 19-inch denim rectangle over flag and
sew around 3 sides with a ¹/₂-inch seam, leaving
left side open. Clip corners (Fig. 4).

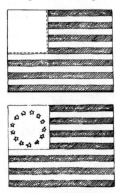

Fig. 3

Fig. 4

Fold 14-inch × 37-inch denim rectangle in half
crosswise, right sides together. Stitch along sides
and clip corners (Fig. 5). Fold denim strips
lengthwise, right sides together, and stitch ¹/₂
inch from edge and turn (Fig. 6). Turn flag right
side out.

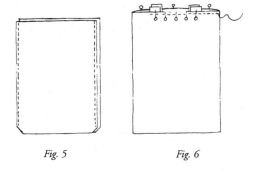

Fig. 5   *Fig. 6*

Pin handles to each side of bag (centered on
each side, about 3 inches apart) and lining over
bag, right sides together (Fig. 7).

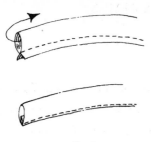

Fig. 7

Stitch around top of bag through handles, leaving 6-inch opening to turn. Turn bag right side out, pushing lining down into bag. Topstitch around upper edge (Fig. 8).

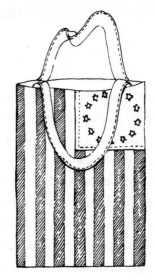

Fig. 8

Sunshine Director's Chairs

———— ❖ ————

*D*irector's chairs are a relatively inexpensive and very versatile furniture option. They look great on decks, porches and patios, and in family rooms and kitchens. The covers can be purchased separately, allowing you to change them according to your taste or to replace them for wear and tear. I've been seeing customized director's chair covers showing up at many summer fairs, along with matching place mats and napkins. These decorator items are usually hand-painted with stencils or stamps. I find fruit prints to be one of the simplest ways to customize a project; I particularly like the effect of printing with lemons, limes, and oranges. When allowed to dry, the citrus fruits develop a texture that makes a perfect paint stamp. Sometimes I'll use a combination of yellow, green, and orange (lemons, limes, and oranges) all in one design. At other times it's more effective to go monochromatic with just one color of fruit. It all depends on the background color of your canvas covers, and the decor you're working with. Actually, there's no rule that says citrus prints have to be the color of the fruit you're using, especially if they're for use indoors. If a kitchen is plum, print plum-colored limes! I was once told by a woman at a crafts fair that she'd sold out of blue lemon print place mats. It turned out that "cornflower" was the most popular Laura Ashley kitchen color that year—seems like everyone had the same wallpaper.

---

lemons, limes, or oranges
fabric paints in desired color(s)
sharp knife
aluminum pie pans
paper towels
director's chair covers in solid colors
coordinating napkins, mats, or table runner
spray fabric protector

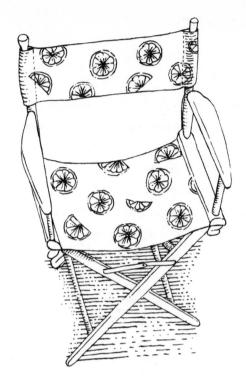

Slice fruit in half, in wedges, or both. Allow to dry out for about two days. Fruit will shrink somewhat and develop more texture for printing. Pour desired color(s) of paint into pan(s) in shallow puddle. Practice printing citrus slices on paper towels. This will help you decide what design to use and how much paint you want to blot off to achieve the desired effect. Print on chair covers, napkins, mats, etc., following manufacturer's directions for setting paint (if necessary).

After paint has dried and set, you may want to coat fabric with a stain protection spray. This is most crucial for director's chair covers, as repeated washing of soiled covers causes them to shrink just enough that they no longer fit the chair frames. If napkins or mats shrink slightly, it's really not a problem.

SEASIDE CANDLESTICKS
MAKES 2

❖

*R*emember when every little neighborhood Italian restaurant had a Chianti bottle in the center of the table? These romantic candle holders were covered with layer upon layer of wax drippings. I rarely see them anymore . . . I guess they seem a bit trite to all the trendy new pizza places. Too bad, because bottles actually make very versatile candlesticks. Visions of those classic Chianti bottles are what inspired this design. I needed a centerpiece (and a light source) for a summer seafood dinner on the deck. Living by the coast, I decided to combine nautical materials. Covering wine bottles with rope and shells turned into a striking solution.

2 wine bottles (Burgundy or Bordeaux)
19 to 21 yards (9$^1/2$ to 10$^1/2$ yards
per bottle) $^3/8$- to $^1/2$-inch manila rope
razor blade
thick craft glue
paintbrush
small seashells (1$^1/2$ inches or less)
pins
2 candles to fit bottle necks
(choose sea colors such as coral or
seafoam green)

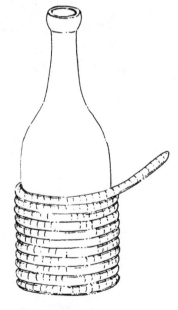

Fig. 1

If desired, soak labels off wine bottles. (This isn't essential, since bottles will be completely covered.) Cut starting end of rope at an angle with razor blade and start wrapping rope around base of each bottle, brushing on glue to about 3 inches up from bottom. It's best to glue a small area at a time, covering it with rope before applying more glue to bottle (Fig. 1).

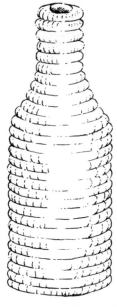

Fig. 2

Continue gluing and wrapping rope a few inches at a time until you reach the top. It helps to anchor rope in place by inserting pins, vertically, through each layer of rope into the row below. Cut final end of rope at an angle with razor. Glue cut edge so that it's tucked neatly against coil. Allow to dry thoroughly (Fig. 2). Glue shells in pleasing pattern around bottles and insert candles (Fig. 3).

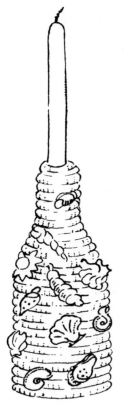

Fig. 3

AUTUMN

❖

Autumn is famed for large state and local country fairs. Traditionally this was the time when farmers gathered to compare the fruits of their harvest. Produce and livestock were judged to be the biggest, the best, or both. People came just to see a 300-pound squash or a bull the size of a buffalo. Craft contests rewarded skills in everything from carving to quilting. This was the place to pick up home furnishings. From blankets and cribs to kitchen cupboards, everything was proudly produced by hand. A century ago, fall fairs were a mecca for rural communities. Farm families made pilgrimages from hundreds of miles away. They were an important social function before the long winter set in. This legacy continues through contemporary times. Fall fairs are now a reason to go for a drive in the country, take in the color of the turning leaves, and sip from jugs of fresh apple cider. The romance of handcrafted items is experiencing a real renaissance. Although country craft fairs will never replace department stores, many people consider them an essential part of their shopping routine. Nowadays fall fairs are an excuse to celebrate everything from cranberries to Indian corn. Foliage and pumpkin fests are by far the most popular, the latter making this orange squash the supreme symbol of autumn.

Autumn

❖

Cinnamon Sachet Apples

Cinnamon-Scented Potpourri

Little Red Schoolhouse Candle Holders

Birdhouse Gourds

Gilded Gourd Box

Calico Pumpkin Pillow

Maple Leaf Wreath With Walnut Pumpkins

Covered Bridge Bird Feeder

Boo Babies

Indian Corn Door Doll

Fall Foliage Shirt

Scroll-Saw Squirrel

Ozark Apple Head Doll

CINNAMON SACHET APPLES
MAKES 8

❖

September is "apple for the teacher" time, and apple crafts abound at country fairs. This age-old tradition is tied into the fall harvest; farm children presented home-grown apples to their instructors as a matter of etiquette. Many believe those days of good manners are gone, but I still see kids bringing small gifts to their teachers. Maybe "apple polishing" is the ulterior motive, but I think it's a nice gesture. Any teacher would welcome these cinnamon-scented versions, stuffed with potpourri and sewn from apple-printed muslin. Every fall I decorate my home by filling a small fruit basket with these. The aroma is wonderful, and the house smells like I'm baking apple pie!

1 large apple
apple red fabric paint
aluminum pie pan
paper towels
$1/4$ yard muslin
scissors
pins
needle
sewing machine (optional)
thread to match muslin
$1^1/4$ yards $3/4$-inch green satin ribbon
thick craft glue
8 cinnamon sticks
small rubber bands
CINNAMON-SCENTED POTPOURRI
(instructions follow)
small fruit basket (optional)*
brown and green acrylic paints
small paintbrush (optional)

Slice apple in half from top to bottom and allow both sides to dry for 24 to 48 hours. (It's important to use both halves because apples are irregular in shape and you want each printed side of fabric to be the mirror image of the other.) Pour shallow puddle of paint into pie pan. Practice printing apple slices on paper towels until you achieve an effect that pleases you. (The print will vary with the number of blottings.) Print with each side of apple 8 times making a total of 16 prints. Allow paint to dry and set according to manufacturer's directions (if necessary). Cut around prints, leaving $1/4$-inch seam allowance (if you are whipstitching apples by hand, leave a $1/8$-inch seam allowance). Keep right and left sides of apples in separate piles so you don't get them mixed up. Pin together opposite prints of apples, printed sides together.

(Continued)

With sewing machine, stitch ¼ inch from edge, leaving 1-inch opening at top to turn where stem will be inserted (Fig. 1). Clip curves. If whipstitching by hand, there's no need to clip curves. Turn apples right side out and press.

Fig. 3

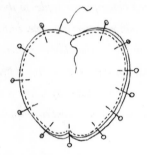

Fig. 1

Prepare leaves and stems: Cut ribbon into approximately 7-inch lengths. Form a loop, crossing ribbon close to ends. (Fig. 2). Glue intersection of

apples about half full with potpourri. Insert stems in holes and stuff more potpourri around stems. Slipstitch opening around stem so it is securely held in place by tightly stitched fabric (Fig. 4).

Fig. 2

ribbon together and wrap around cinnamon stick, gluing in place. Use small rubber band to hold ribbon in position while it dries (Fig. 3). Stuff

Fig. 4

NOTE: If you are using a fruit basket, choose one in the style of a classic peck basket. Print apples on side of basket while you're printing fabric. Add stem and leaf to each apple with paint and brush.

Opposite: Seaside Candlesticks, page 60

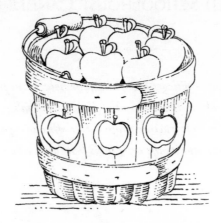

Fig. 5

CINNAMON-SCENTED POTPOURRI
MAKES ABOUT 4 CUPS

1½ cups dried rose petals
1½ cups cedar shavings
½ cup chopped dried orange peel
½ cup coarsely crushed cinnamon sticks
¼ cup coarsely crushed whole nutmeg
1 teaspoon orrisroot powder*
6 to 8 drops concentrated cinnamon oil

Toss together and store in airtight container. Makes enough for about 8 apples.

NOTE: Look for orrisroot powder at a nursery or crafts store or in the floral department of a supermarket.

Opposite: Cinnamon Sachet Apples, page 65
With Cinnamon-Scented Potpourri, page 67

LITTLE RED SCHOOLHOUSE CANDLE HOLDERS
MAKES 2

❖

*A*t fall fairs I often see entire villages of wood candle holders cut from pine blocks. They're really quite attractive when displayed on the dining room table or sideboard. You can paint them to look like any type of structure, from a post office to a general store. However, I'm partial to red schoolhouses. Perhaps it's the little brass bell (or maybe it's just that they work well with my wallpaper).

two 4-inch square blocks cut from
2-inch × 4-inch pine stock
pencil
triangle
cross-cut saw
auger with 1-inch bit
vise
sandpaper
barn red wood stain
rag
acrylic paints: dark gray, yellow ochre, white,
peach, slate blue, brown, grass green
detail brushes
fine-point red and black permanent-ink
felt-tip markers
matte acrylic sealer
1¹/₂-inch flat paintbrush
small screw-in hook
¹/₂-inch bell
two 10-inch taper candles

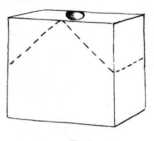

Fig. 1

Place blocks in vise and drill 2-inch-deep hole in center top with auger. At center of block, mark a 45° angle for roof pitch and cut with saw; hole will be in center (Fig. 1). Sand blocks smooth. Stain red with rag and allow to dry. Paint details on block with acrylic paints: First paint roof dark gray making scalloped shingles at edges. Paint door gray (Fig. 2). Paint yellow ochre for windows

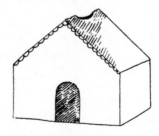

Fig. 2

Fig. 3

Draw eyes on children with black pen and mouths with red pen. Paint green blades of grass around base of blocks. Coat with acrylic sealer. Screw in hook and hang bell over sign. Fit candles in holes (Fig. 5).

(Fig. 3). Paint stylized children on each side of door. Use peach paint for face and arms, blue for overalls and dress. Paint shoes brown and hair brown or ochre (Fig. 4). Allow to dry. Outline windows and door frame with white. Paint picket fence around back and sides of school in white. Use white to make sign over door. Allow to dry. Use black pen to outline features on house

Fig. 4

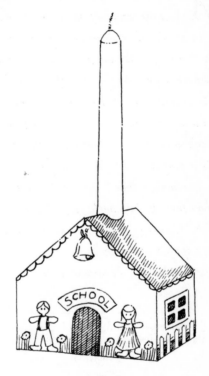

Fig. 5

and to accent roof shingles, door slats, and doorknob. Write *SCHOOL* or *SCHOOLHOUSE* on sign.

BIRDHOUSE GOURDS
MAKES 2

❖

*M*artins have been farmers' friends since the dawn of agriculture. A single martin will eat about 80 pounds of insects in six months. That's why gardeners often try to encourage martins to take up residence on their property. They live in colonies and require multiple dwelling units. Long before you could buy fancy martin apartment buildings for your backyard, Native Americans understood the value of these birds; they made martin houses out of gourds. When brightly painted gourds hang clustered in a tree, they resemble year-round Christmas ornaments. Any type of martin complex needs to be mounted high off the ground (at least 15 feet) to attract occupants. It will take a minimum of 6 gourds to attract a colony of martins—the more, the merrier! Gourds also make appealing shelters for wrens. But wrens require more personal space; limit gourds for wren houses to no more than 3 per acre. The best gourds for birdhouses are smooth "dipper" gourds, as well as those from the **Lagenaria** genus. Of course, many seed catalogs specifically market "birdhouse gourds." Growing gourds is a rewarding, almost amusing experience. When you plant a mixed seed packet of ornamental gourds, you never know what silly shapes will pop up. I've included some gourd growing basics with the birdhouse directions in case you want to cultivate your own.

"birdhouse" gourds (pear-shaped and smooth-sided specimens) thoroughly dried *
pencil
compass
drill with 1/8-inch bit
craft knife with narrow serrated blade
wood filler
sandpaper
aluminum foil
acrylic paints: assorted colors
1-inch flat paintbrush and detail brushes
matte acrylic sealer
copper wire

Prepare several gourds and plan to hang them in a grouping in order to attract a colony of martins. Mark a spot about 3/4 inch from top of gourd for drilling hole. Drill completely through to other

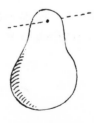

Fig. 1

side of gourd neck (Fig. 1). Draw a 1-inch circle in side of gourd using pencil and compass. Drill hole just inside circle; do not drill through opposite side of gourd (Fig. 2). This hole is to get the craft

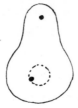

Fig. 2

knife started. Cut out circle along penciled line using sawing motion. Remove any fibers from inside gourd. Fill cracks with wood filler. Allow to dry, then sand smooth.

Painting gourds is the fun part. You can make them all the same or completely different. Cover work surface with aluminum foil to keep gourds from sticking. Start with 2 base coats of a solid color. From there you can paint stripes (Fig. 3), polka dots (Fig. 4), or even paint the gourd to look like a little house complete with picket fence (Fig. 5). Coat with a layer of acrylic sealer.

Hang gourds by stringing a length of copper wire through holes in neck.

Fig. 3

Fig. 4

Fig. 5

NOTE: Try growing your own gourds! It's really quite simple and satisfying. Plant gourd seeds two or three weeks after the average date of the last killing frost. Choose a sunny spot and prepare the ground with a spade, or till deeply. Rake smooth and sow seeds every 3 feet. Drop 5 seeds in a ring about 2 inches in diameter (called a "hill"). Cover seeds with 1/2-inch of soil. When plants are about 2 inches tall, thin each hill to 2 plants. Although gourd vines can run along the ground, you'll have nicer specimens if you provide a trellis or wire fence for the plants to climb. Gourds must be thoroughly matured on the vine before picking, or they will decay. Pick gourds when the vine is dry and withered, leaving a piece of stem at the top of the gourd. They must be harvested before the first frost and allowed to dry in a cool dry place for several weeks.

GILDED GOURD BOX
MAKES 2

❖

*H*ere's another gourd project—it just wouldn't be fall without them. This time of year, country fairs are filled with gourd crafts. There are historical reasons for this. Thousands of years ago, gourds became one of man's first tools. When properly dried, they could be hollowed out and used for bottles, bowls, and spoons. Today's craftsmen still look to gourds for creative possibilities. I remember walking into my favorite garden center and spotting a whimsical golden box on the counter. It was made from a large gourd, covered with autumn leaves and gilded antique gold. I asked the store manager where she got it and she said: "A customer grew it from seed and brought it back as a gift." All I can say is that an ordinary gourd had been transformed into a treasure. It reminded me of another metamorphosis . . . when a plain pumpkin turned into Cinderella's golden carriage.

That year I experimented with decoupaging leaves to gourds to be "gold leafed." I learned a few things in the process. For starters, there's no point in using leaves that have already fallen off the trees. Flexible, fresh-picked leaves are easier to apply and less likely to crack or be filled with holes. Smaller leaves conform more easily to the curved sides of a gourd. Once glued to the gourd, they need time to dry out. Timing is essential to this project. You need to collect the earliest harvest of gourds available, while your local leaves are barely tinged with color. These won't be as brittle and difficult to work with.

smooth-surfaced flat gourds, thoroughly dried (also see BIRDHOUSE GOURDS, page 70, for growing tips)	acrylic polymer
	craft brushes
	small maple or oak leaves, freshly picked
pencil	acrylic paint (cadmium or crimson red and black)
drill with 1/8-inch bit	aluminum foil
craft knife with narrow serrated blade	antique gold spray paint
wood filler	spray acrylic sealer
sandpaper	

Mark a circle around top half of gourd with pencil to form lid. (Depending on type of gourd, there may be a natural seam that defines a lid.) Drill a hole along line to get knife started (Fig. 1).

Fig. 1

Cut around line with craft knife, using sawing motion. Remove lid and pull any fibers out of gourd. Fill any holes in gourd's surface with wood filler. Allow to dry and sand smooth. Coat the surface of gourd with acrylic polymer and firmly press leaves onto surface, smoothing out air bubbles (Fig. 2); polymer dries quickly,

so work on a small area at a time. Allow leaves to dry on gourd for several days, then apply two more coats of polymer. When last coat of polymer is dry, paint outside of gourd red, and inside black. Place gourd base and lid on aluminum foil, cavity side down, and spray with gold paint. (It's okay if crackles of red show through—in fact, that's the desired effect.) When paint is dry, coat with a spray of acrylic sealer. Once outside has dried, coat inside with sealer (Fig. 3).

Fig. 3

Fig. 2

CALICO PUMPKIN PILLOW
MAKES 1 LARGE OR 2 SMALL

❖

Pumpkin pillows are the most popular craft item at fall country fairs. They come in all sizes and sometimes wear witches' hats. But I prefer not to appliqué jack o'lantern faces on them, because plain pumpkin pillows can be used into the Thanksgiving holiday season. I've even seen some that were filled with aquarium gravel in addition to stuffing. They become as heavy as the real thing and make great doorstops.

1/2 yard orange calico fabric
4-inch × 8-inch strip of brown burlap
pins
needle
thread (to match calico and burlap)
cotton or polyester stuffing
sewing machine

Enlarge pattern to scale. You can also make the pumpkin pillows half size by using pattern at present scale and cut enough panels for two smaller pumpkins. Use pattern to cut 12 panels from fabric. Because you'll be sewing many panels together, it's important to keep seams aligned with each panel as you work. Mark notches from pattern on each panel and be sure that they line up, since the top of the pumpkin will be slightly smaller than the base. Begin by pinning 6 sets of 2 panels each, right sides together. For larger pumpkins, stitch 1/2 inch from edge, starting and stopping 1/2 inch from beginning and ending of seams. Smaller pumpkins require 1/4 inch seams, starting and stopping 1/4 inch from beginning and ending of seams. Back stitch starting and stopping points to reinforce. This is important to remember when joining all panels. Pin 3 sets of double panels together and join at seams. You'll now have a hemisphere shape resembling an inside-out beach ball (Fig. 1).

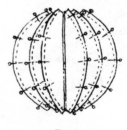

Fig. 1

Repeat with remaining sets of 3 double panels. To ease tension at intersections, clip seams up to (but not through) stitching lines at the center

Opposite: Birdhouse Gourds, page 70

top and center bottom. Pin both halves right sides together and sew around seam allowing a 4-inch opening to turn (2-inch for small pumpkins). Turn fabric through opening. For stem: Fold burlap in half lengthwise. Press. Stitch along unfolded edge. Begin rolling up like cinnamon stick until you reach desired stem diameter (Fig. 2).

Slipstitch through rolled layers of burlap to stabilize the stem (Fig. 3). Place base of stem at

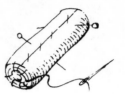

Fig. 3

Fig. 2

top of pumpkin. Sew securely in place by reaching inside opening of pillow. Fill with stuffing and slipstitch opening (Fig. 4).

(Thicker stems look best on larger pillows, thinner stems on smaller ones.) Cut burlap and tuck raw edge under. Slipstitch in place.

Fig. 4

(Continued)

Opposite: *Calico Pumpkin Pillow, page 74*

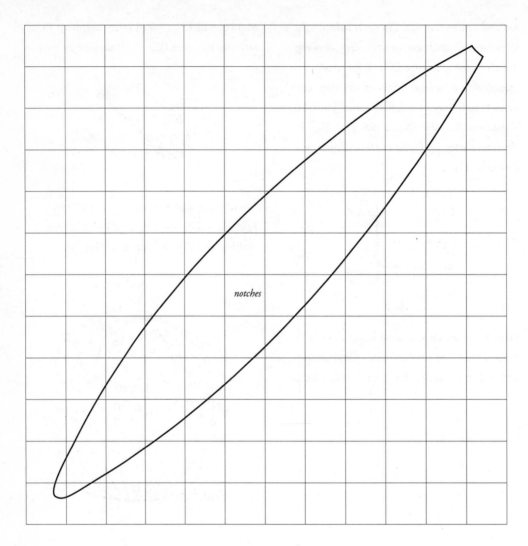

notches

1 square = 1 inch

Maple Leaf Wreath With Walnut Pumpkins
MAKES 1

❖

This fall foliage wreath captures the essence of autumn with preserved leaves and quaint walnut pumpkins. For best results, pick leaves while they're fresh and vibrant, before they begin to brown. If your timing isn't right, you can still use silk maple leaves.

16 walnuts
aluminum foil
pumpkin orange acrylic paint
paintbrush
thick craft glue
hot glue gun
16 whole cloves
4 yards each ¼-inch orange, red,
and yellow satin ribbon
10- or 12-inch grapevine wreath
preserved* or silk maple leaves in assorted
colors and sizes

Fig. 1

Place walnuts on sheet of aluminum foil and paint one side orange. When paint is dry, turn walnuts over and paint underside. Remove ball from clove stems. When walnuts are painted and completely dry, use craft glue to attach cloves for "stems." Allow glue to dry (Fig. 1). Hold ribbons together and wrap around grapevine wreath. Use extra streamers to tie into

(Continued)

multiloop bow (Fig. 2). Use hot glue gun to attach walnut pumpkins around wreath. Weave stems of maple leaves into vines and ribbons.

Trim stems when necessary and anchor leaves in place with drop of craft glue (Fig. 3).

Fig. 2

Fig. 3

NOTE: Preserve leaves by gathering small branches of maple (or oak) leaves at the peak of color. Cut base of each stem at an angle. Make a mixture of 40 percent glycerine and 60 percent almost-boiling water. Fill vases half full with the solution and place stems in them. Allow leaves to dry in a cool, dark room for a week or two, depending on humidity. It's normal for leaves preserved by this method to darken. Dried leaves that have been pressed between the pages of a heavy book may also be used. However, these will be very flat and inflexible. If you plan to press your own leaves, start collecting them this fall for next fall.

COVERED BRIDGE BIRD FEEDER
MAKES 1

—◆—

*I*n the northwest corner of Connecticut there's a quintessential country town called West Cornwall. Here one can see possibly the world's most photographed covered bridge. Weekenders from New York come in droves to try to drive across it. This can take all afternoon, since it's a one-car bridge (so visiting is not always a good idea during fall foliage season!). But to really appreciate a covered bridge one has to take the time to walk through it. As you enter, imagine how you might feel being a frightened horse with blinders on. Wouldn't you rather walk into a cozy barn than traverse a rushing stream? Alas, these precious pieces of Americana really did disappear with the horse and buggy. Still, the symbol will live forever in our hearts. I think this miniature covered bridge makes an inspired bird feeder, spanning a stone wall, tree limb, or stockade fence. This is definitely a project for a woodworker—but there's no need for professional power tools, just basic equipment simple enough for beginners. One important thing to remember about purchasing lumber: it's not actually the size you buy. For example, 1-inch × 6-inch boards are really $3/4$ inch × $5^1/2$ inches, 1-inch × 4-inch boards are really $3/4$ inch × $3^1/2$ inches. Most boards are available in 4-, 6-, or 8-foot lengths. Rough-sawn cedar will give the best "old bridge" effect, but it may not be as easy to find as pressure-treated (green) pine.

27 inches of 1-inch × 6-inch and 38 inches of 1-inch × 4-inch cedar or pressure-treated pine. (Boards come in 6- or 8-foot lengths.) yardstick pencil crosscut saw scroll saw hammer rasp	sand paper 4d zinc-plated finishing nails $3/4$-inch × 10-inch brass piano hinge with screws small screwdriver barn red wood stain wood sealer rag $1^1/2$-inch flat paintbrush

(Continued)

With crosscut saw, cut one 15-inch length (for bridge base) and two 5 1/4-inch lengths (for ends) from a 1-inch × 6-inch board (which is actually 3/4 inch × 5 1/2 inches). Cut two 8 1/2-inch lengths (for sides) and two 10-inch lengths (for roof) from a 1-inch × 4-inch board (which is actually 3/4 inch × 3 1/2 inches).

Enlarge pattern for ends of bridge to scale, and transfer onto 5 1/4-inch × 5 1/2-inch pieces. Cut angle of roof with crosscut saw and cut out opening with scroll saw. Sand all rough edges of wood. Use rasp to make vertical grooves along sides, ends, and roof pieces to resemble barn siding. Nail sides to ends, anchoring in place with about 3 nails on each side of each end (Fig. 1).

Fig. 2

aligning edge with center and using 3 nails on each side. Screw in piano hinge along roof seam, allowing one side to open and shut freely so that it can be filled with birdseed. Stain barn red with rag. Allow to dry. Brush on two coats of wood sealer, allowing to dry between coats (Fig. 3).

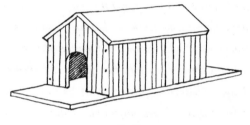

Fig. 3

Fig. 1

Center bridge on base and nail base to bridge from the bottom, using about 7 nails through each side (Fig. 2). Nail one side of roof to top of bridge,

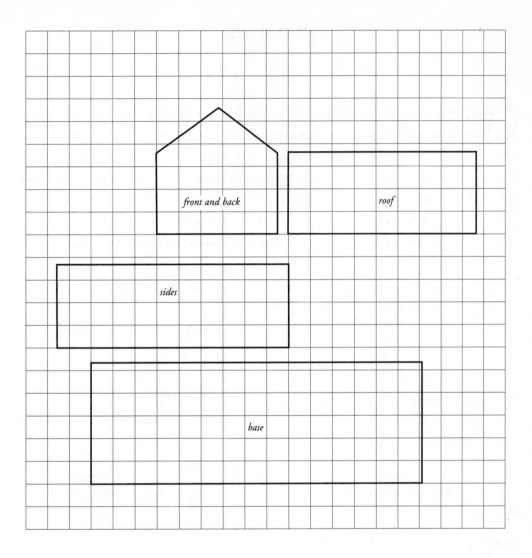

front and back

roof

sides

base

1 square = 1 inch

BOO BABIES
MAKES 3

❖

*O*ctoberfests, pumpkin fests, and Halloween "haunted houses" are filled with crafts from the "world beyond." Whether you're hunting wicked witch vacuum cleaner covers or skeleton coat racks, evil spirits abound. But some are rather innocent looking. Take, for instance, "boo babies." They remind me of that old cartoon, **Casper the Friendly Ghost.** These soft, squooshy, not-so-spooky pillow toys are nothing more than a creatively stuffed T-shirt. In fact, infants love snuggling up to them—while they'll often burst into tears at the sight of a jack o'lantern. The instructions are for a collection of three dolls in small, medium, and large. Construction is essentially the same for all sizes.

white T-shirts: infant's (for 7-inch doll),
boy's (for 9-inch doll) and man's large
(for 14-inch doll)
needle
white thread
cotton or polyester stuffing
¹/₂ yard elastic cord
about 1¹/₂ yards 1-inch ruffled lace or
eyelet trim
about 1¹/₄ to 1¹/₂ yards each ¹/₂ inch
black and orange satin ribbon
scissors
pins
black embroidery floss

Fig. 1

Fig. 2

Wash and dry shirts to preshrink. For each doll: slipstitch bottom edges of shirt together (Fig. 1). Tie bottom corners of shirt and sleeves in tight knots. Fill with stuffing (Fig. 2). Make head by pulling up crew neck and tying tightly with

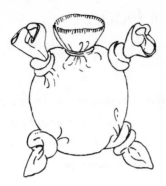

Fig. 3

floss to make eyes. (Connect eyes by pulling through head and indenting slightly.) Cut ribbon into 3 equal sections of each color. Hold an orange and black ribbon together and tie in tight knot around neck, covering elastic cord. Tie ribbons in bow adjusting size of bow and trimming ends to desired length in scale to doll's size (Fig. 5).

piece of elastic cord about 2¹/₂ inches from top. Fill head with stuffing (Fig. 3). Cut length of lace to fit inside neckline. Pin lace between front and back ribbing and slipstitch in place (Fig. 4). Fold neckline around head to resemble a bonnet and slipstitch in place. Use black embroidery

Fig. 5

Fig. 4

Indian Corn Door Doll
MAKES 1

❖

*O*ne harbinger of the harvest season is a cluster of Indian corn hanging on the front door. It usually stays up until it's time for the Christmas wreath. Country fairs often feature creative variations on this theme. My favorite is a doll with corn husk hair and a calico dress. It can be displayed alone or wired into an arrangement of Indian corn and bittersweet.

1 large ear Indian corn with long husks
2/3 yard 1/4-inch grosgrain ribbon
bowl
paper towel
rubber band
hot glue gun
thick craft glue
7-inch × 24-inch strip of calico fabric
in a fall color
scissors
scalloped pinking shears
floral wire
5 small black shoe buttons
scrap of red felt
straw doll hat

Fig. 1

Carefully pull several strands of corn husks down along sides of corn (husks will be brittle). Cut ribbon into two 6-inch pieces and one 12-inch piece. Tie 6-inch pieces around corn husks on each side, forming ponytails. Trim ponytails and cut remaining husks about 3/4 inch from base (Fig. 1). Soak cut husks in bowl of hot water until soft and flexible. Twist tightly together, wringing out water. Using strands of corn husks, bind bunch together at ends and in the center and trim ragged edges (Fig. 2). Allow to dry on paper towel for 24 hours. (This bunch will be the doll's arms.) Center arms about halfway down front of corn and hot glue in place. Secure with

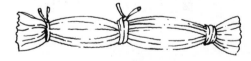

Fig. 2

rubber band (Fig. 3). Prepare dress by cutting
2-inch × 7-inch strip off end of fabric (for sash)
and pinking edges of the 7-inch × 22-inch piece.
Fold fabric in half and cut hole in center, large

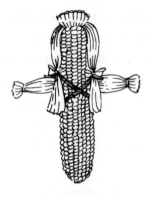

Fig. 3

enough to slip over doll's head. When hot glue is
set, remove rubber band from arms. Twist ends of
floral wire around base of arms. Pull wire tightly
around to center back of doll, twisting several
times to form loop. (Loop should be pressed flat
against corn so it will slip through neckline of

dress.) Press lengthwise edges of sash toward wrong
side. Fold in half lengthwise, wrong sides together.
Press. Slip dress over head, allowing front and back
to fall over arms. Pull in dress under arms, forming
waistline. Tightly wrap sash around waist, securing
with hot glue. Use craft glue to attach two buttons
to face for eyes and three down front of dress. Cut
a small piece from red felt to resemble lips. Glue
on face. Tie remaining 12-inch grosgrain ribbon
around crown of hat. Finish with bow. Hot glue
hat to head (Fig. 4).

Fig. 4

FALL FOLIAGE SHIRT
MAKES 1

———————— ❖ ————————

I've seen this concept executed on T-shirts, oxford cloth men's shirts, and sweatshirts. Assorted fall leaves (particularly maple and oak) are dipped in fabric paint and pressed onto the shirt, creating a beautiful natural print. This time of year, sweatshirts are the practical choice. Cotton-polyester blends are the most colorfast surface, and a black shirt is especially striking, bringing out the fall colors of the print. Be sure to follow the manufacturer's directions on fabric paint; it's often necessary to iron the dried paint to set the colors into the fabric. (And it's wise to hand-wash painted clothing in cold water.) For best results, use leaves that are still somewhat green and flexible.

shirt board*
aluminum foil
cotton-polyester blend T-shirt, sweatshirt,
or oxford cloth shirt
fabric paints: olive, brown,
russet, gold, orange
aluminum pie pans
sponge
assorted fall leaves: oak, maple, elm, etc.
paper towels

Cover shirt board with foil and slip inside shirt to stabilize fabric and keep paint from bleeding through to other side. Pour puddles of paint into separate pie pans. Place each leaf, veined side up, on a towel. Lightly sponge paint onto leaf. Practice printing on additional paper towels to decide how much paint should be blotted off to achieve desired effect. Leaves should be layered according to color. Print olive and brown first; after this layer dries, print russet. Print gold and orange last. Allow to dry. Set paint according to manufacturer's directions (if necessary).

NOTE: Shirt boards are cardboard forms that slip inside knit shirts to stabilize the fabric while it's being painted. They are available at fabric and craft stores. You can also cut your own out of sturdy cardboard.

Scroll-Saw Squirrel
Makes 1

❖

Dummy boards and cutout wood figures are big sellers at country fairs. You can find a full-size Holstein cow for your front yard, or a kitten to curl up by your fireplace. If you have friends who collect these, then you already know they make wonderful gifts. I came up with the inspiration for this one day while watching a squirrel raid my backyard bird feeder. He had a big walnut in his mouth, so I decided to glue a real walnut to the paws of this scroll-saw version. The eyes are sunflower seeds—which, as every bird lover knows, are a squirrel's favorite food!

15 inches of 1-inch × 10-inch pressure-treated
pine board (Boards come in 6- or
8-foot lengths.)
pencil
scroll saw
rasp
hammer
wood glue
4d finishing nails
vise
sandpaper
gray wood stain
rag
spray- or brush-on acrylic sealer
2 sunflower seeds
permanent-ink black felt tip marker
walnut

and 2 leg pieces, cutting along lines with scroll saw. Be sure to mark insides of legs (Fig. 1).

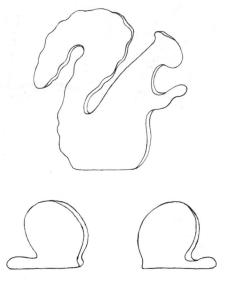

Fig. 1

Enlarge pattern to scale and transfer onto pine board. (Do this with transfer paper, or cut out pattern and draw around pieces.) Cut 1 body

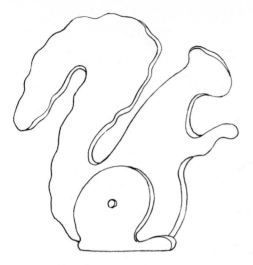

Fig. 2

Fig. 3

File outsides of legs and outer edges of both sides of body with rasp to soften edges. Sand surfaces until smooth. Apply glue to insides of legs and glue to each side of leg. Hammer a nail into side of each leg (Fig. 2). Clamp firmly in vise and allow to dry thoroughly. Stain gray with rag. Use marker to draw pupils on sunflower seeds. Glue one seed on each side of head for eyes, and glue walnut in paws (Fig. 3).

(Continued)

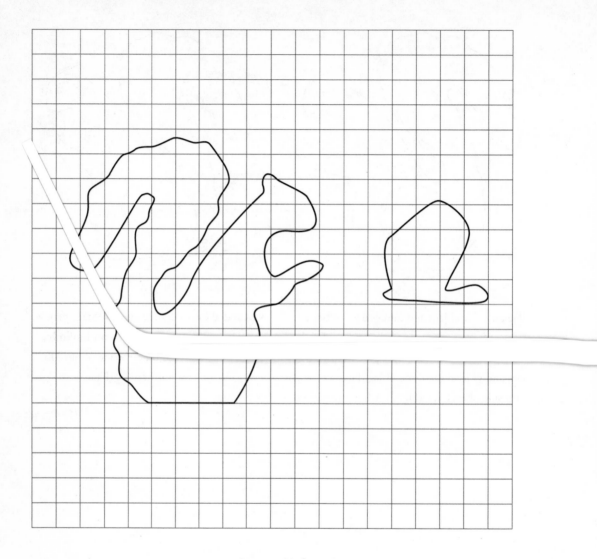

1 square = 1 inch

*Opposite: Maple Leaf Wreath
With Walnut Pumpkins, page 77*

OZARK APPLE HEAD DOLL
MAKES 1

——— ❖ ———

*I remember visiting Silver Dollar City, in the heart of the Ozarks as a little girl on a crisp autumn day. It was one of the granddaddies of modern-day theme parks, and a charming place for children. I took a ride on an antique train, wore a coonskin cap, and ate beef stew out of a tin cup in a "mining camp." Most of all, I remember Mom buying the ugliest doll I'd ever seen. Apple head dolls were one of the region's famous crafts and a "must have" souvenir. As the years went by, the doll's face just grew older and older, with more and more wrinkles. It even started getting age spots! (Then again, perhaps it was mildew. We'd moved to a house by the water.) The shriveled-up head used to bother me, but my brother thought it was **cool**. (It reminded him of a witch doctor's shrunken head.) One year the head got so small, it practically disappeared! I was in college by then, and I knew it was time to say good-bye to the ugly old apple head doll. After all, it had lived a long, full life. Every time I looked at it, it brought me back to a special time and place when I was at the ultimate country fair.*

three 2¹/₂-inch diameter apples
salt
paring knife
whole cloves
¹/₂ cup lemon juice
16-gauge copper wire
wire cutters
pliers
powder blush
spray acrylic sealer
roll of first-aid cotton
white thread
leg from ladies' stockings or panty hose, nude or suntan, and thread to match
6-inch square scraps of white cotton knit and blue denim (old T-shirts and jeans are good sources)

4-inch square scrap of brown or black faux suede or felt, and thread to match
scissors
pins
needle
sewing machine (optional)
¹/₄ yard ¹/₄-inch red grosgrain ribbon
four ¹/₈-inch buttons
thick craft glue
hot glue gun
straw doll hat
scrap of red bandanna or calico fabric
tree stump*

(Continued)

Opposite: Boo Babies, page 82

There's no predicting the ultimate expression on an apple head doll. That's why you need to prepare 3 apples for every doll you make—you'll have more options to choose from. Pare apples, leaving 3/4-inch circle of peel at both ends of core. Scrape surface smooth. With knife point, mark placement of eyes, nose, and mouth. Sculpt nose first by carving away some apple underneath and along the sides. Hollow out eye sockets and cut a smiling gash for mouth (Fig. 1).

Fig. 2

Fig. 1

Dip heads in lemon juice and coat with salt to accelerate drying process. Cut three 10-inch lengths of copper wire with wire cutters. Poke a wire through core of each apple. Bend wire at bottom to keep apple from falling off, and make hook at top. Insert cloves in eye sockets. (Fig. 2). Hang apples in a cool, dry place away from direct sunlight for several months or until apple is shriveled to about 2/3 its original size and the surface is dry, leathery and

wrinkled. Dust blusher on cheeks and nose. Spray with acrylic sealer.

Make wire frame for body by cutting 35-inch length of copper wire. Fold in half. Twist wire halfway down. Fold back free ends to form 1 1/2-inch loops for feet. Cut 15-inch length of wire and twist middle around body frame, 2 inches from top. Fold back free ends of wire to form 3/4-inch loops for hands (Fig. 3). Wrap

Fig. 3

Fig. 4

sheets of cotton around body, arms, and legs, securing in place with white thread. Wrap body so it's thicker than arms and legs (Fig. 4). Cut 12-inch tube from stocking; pull over legs and body. Cut side slits for armholes. Turn raw edges under and slipstitch over shoulders. Slit tube between legs. Turn in raw edges and slipstitch around each leg, trimming ends to meet edges of feet. Turn under raw edges and slipstitch. Cut 2 strips from stocking,

about 5½ inches × 2 inches. Wrap around arms and hands, slipstitching seams and sewing to body (Fig. 5).

There are no exact patterns for shirt, overalls, and boots, because there's no telling what size your doll will be after you finish stuffing it. (It could be on the fat side or the thin side.) The best way to get a custom fit is to simply pin fabric around doll, trim to seam allowance of ¼ inch and stitch pieces, right sides together. Turn clothes right side out and put on doll. For shirt: Make ½-inch slit in center of cotton knit square and pull over neck. Pin around body and under arms. Trim to seam allowance, adjusting sleeve length if desired. Do the same with scraps of faux suede around feet for boots (Fig. 6). Sew seams, right sides together, ¼ inch from edge on sewing machine; clip curves (Fig. 7). If whipstitching by hand, trim seam allowance to ⅛ inch. Turn

Fig. 5

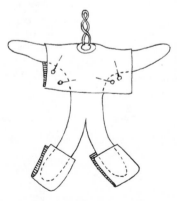

Fig. 6

(Continued)

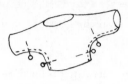

Fig. 7

clothing right side out and put on doll. For pants: Cut denim into two 3-inch × 7-inch strips. Pin around back and front of doll and between legs. Cut slit between legs and mark stitching line with pencil, allowing a 1/4- to 1/8-inch seam allowance (Fig. 8). Remove from doll and sew pants right sides together, at side seams and between legs. Turn right side out. Turn waist under 1/4 inch and topstitch. Fray hem of pants (Fig. 9). Put pants on doll. Cut ribbon

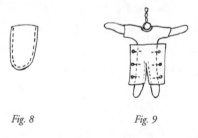

Fig. 8   *Fig. 9*

to length of suspenders and pin in place at insides of waistband at front and back, crossing in back. Sew buttons through front of pants to anchor suspenders in place. Select your

favorite apple head and push into frame on exposed wire (secure in place with hot glue gun). Shred up some cotton and apply to head with thick craft glue. Twist wisps of cotton for eyebrows and moustache. Glue in place with craft glue. When dry, glue on straw hat. Cut triangular scarf from red bandanna fabric and tie around neck. Bend so doll can sit on stump. If desired, anchor in place with hot glue gun (Fig. 10). Fold hands in lap, or put small object such as a miniature pipe or fishing pole in hands.

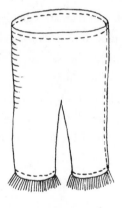

Fig. 10

Fig. 11

NOTE: For stump, cut a 3-inch slice from a 3- to 4-inch-diameter tree branch. Use a crosscut saw and sand cut edges.

HELPFUL HINT: If you don't have months of patience to wait for apple heads to dry, it can be done in the oven. The trick is having a reliable low-temperature setting. The oven must *never* go above 160°F (70°C) or the end result will be mushy baked apples. Wire apples to upper oven rack, and place a dark-colored roasting pan on lowest rack to catch drippings and diffuse heat. Dry apples on lowest possible oven setting for 5 to 6 days.

WINTER

❖

Come the winter holidays, country fairs go indoors to school, church, and community auditoriums. Here in Connecticut it's not unusual to have a bazaar in a barn. At a "Yankee barn sale" the sweet smells of sugar, spice, and fresh-cut Christmas trees draw you through the door. Inside there's a visual candyland that makes even the most "adult" adult feel like a little kid. Creative bakers and craftsmen have filled the place with home-baked goodies, handmade gifts, and original ornaments. Many of these country-inspired crafts borrow from materials in nature. Pinecones, branches, bay leaves, berries, cinnamon sticks, and seashells all find their way into this Christmas collection. Historically, this is why we have winter holidays. How else could man's spirit survive the long days of darkness and bitter chill? This is a time when northern cultures honed their craftsmanship, from intricate embroideries to hand-carved cuckoo clocks. That's why we bring trees indoors—to create our own festival of lights and color. The only trouble is that Christmas comes too soon. It's over before the last dry pine needle is out the door . . . long before the real winter doldrums set in. Perhaps this is why we have Valentine's Day! What better motivation to keep us going than chocolate? This holiday helps melt the ice with sinfully rich chocolate festivals and sweetheart bazaars.

Winter

❖

Pinecone Table Turkeys

Bay Leaf Spice Wreath

Artichoke Trees

Pinecone Christmas Trees

Cinn-a-men Wreath

Honeybee Potpourri Wreaths

Silver Bell Scallop Shells

Baker's Clay Christmas Trees

Cornstarch Casting Clay for Cookie Molds

Scottie Tree Skirt

Necktie Teddy

Puss in Boots Stocking

Rover Wreath

Nutcracker Christmas Box

Stuffed Sock Snowmen

Be Mine Rosebuds

Sweetheart Sachets

Rose Petal Potpourri

PINECONE TABLE TURKEYS
MAKES 8

❖

Thanksgiving is a transitional time: Is it still fall, or is it the harbinger of the holidays? Actually, it's both. Aside from family dinners and TV football, Thanksgiving will be experienced differently in different climates. The leaves are long gone in New England, while remnants of autumn remain in the South. In the West it's hard to imagine that winter's even on the way. For this reason, many of the pumpkin crafts from the previous chapter are perfect for Thanksgiving decorations. However, I thought it was only appropriate to start off the winter chapter with "table turkeys"—an attractive and amusing way to mark place settings at your Thanksgiving gathering. Kids and relatives love them, and they score as take-home souvenirs (even if your sweet potatoes don't).

tree limb section, 3 to 3¹/₂ inches in diameter
ruler
pencil
crosscut saw
vise
sandpaper
hot glue gun
thick craft glue
8 4-inch pinecones
8 whole almonds, 8 almond slivers
8 dried bittersweet berries
natural colored hobby feathers, 2¹/₂ to
4 inches long
four 3¹/₄-inch × 5⁷/₈-inch ice cream sticks
craft knife
black, fine-point black permanent-ink
felt-tip marker

Mark limb into eight ³/₄- to 1-inch sections. Saw into discs. Sand cut sides, leaving bark around edges. Use hot glue gun to attach one pinecone horizontally to each wood base. Hot glue almond just above narrow end of pinecone, with natural seam around almond positioned vertically in relation to pinecone (Fig. 1).

Fig. 1

(Continued)

Use craft glue to attach almond sliver beak. Glue dried bittersweet berry underneath. Insert feathers into rear segments of pinecone, gluing in place with craft glue. Trim off rounded edges of craft sticks and cut each into two 2¹/₂-inch lengths. With marker, draw eyes on almonds and write names of dinner guests on ice cream sticks. (If these are to be sold at a bazaar, leave signs blank to be filled in.) Anchor signs at base in front of turkeys with craft glue or glue gun (Fig. 2).

Fig. 2

Bay Leaf Spice Wreath
MAKES 1

❖

*B*uy bay leaves in bulk packages from a restaurant supplier or wholesale club. It's easy to make your own dried orange slices in the microwave: Cut oranges into ¼-inch slices and arrange on a layer of paper towels. Microwave on high for 3 minutes, repeating as necessary until completely dry.

8-, 9-, or 10-inch grapevine wreath
bay leaves
hot glue gun
scissors
1 yard each red and green ¼-inch satin ribbon
6 to 12 whole cinnamon sticks
6 to 9 dried orange slices
8 inches picture wire

Use glue gun to cover vine wreath with bay leaves, overlapping leaves as you work (Fig. 1). Cut ribbon into 6-inch lengths and tie cinnamon sticks to exposed branches of wreath. Tie ribbon ends in bows. Arrange orange slices around wreath and anchor in place with hot glue gun (Fig. 2). Twist picture wire across back of wreath, forming loop for hanging.

Fig. 2

Fig. 1

ARTICHOKE TREES
MAKES 4

❖

These make unique and elegant ornaments for a table, sideboard, or mantle. The dried artichokes are equally dramatic in gold or silver. I like to glue little pearl beads to the spiny tips of the artichoke leaves. Important points to remember: Buy large artichokes (they shrink significantly) and plan ahead (they take nearly a month to dry).

4 large artichokes with long stems
ice pick
scissors
string
gold or silver spray paint
aluminum foil
3-inch or 4-inch clay pots (depending
on size of artichokes)
oasis or floral foam
knife
hot glue gun
Spanish moss
pearl beads (optional)
toothpicks
thick craft glue
3 yards 1-inch wired gold or silver ribbon

Use ice pick to pierce a hole through the side of each artichoke stem. Cut 4 lengths of string about 2 feet long. Thread each piece of string through the hole in an artichoke stem and then wrap around them, ending with a knot. Hang artichokes in a cool, dry place for nearly a month until dry. Cut string from stems and place artichokes on foil.

Spray artichokes with a light coat of paint. When dry, turn artichokes and keep repeating the painting process until artichokes are evenly covered. Cut chunks of oasis or foam that will fit into pots. Push oasis into pot and use knife to hollow out a channel down the center of the oasis that will accommodate the artichoke stem. Use hot glue gun to cover the top of foam (surrounding the hole) with moss. Cover artichoke stem with hot glue and insert into hole. If desired, apply a small amount of craft glue to the hole of a pearl bead, using a toothpick tip. Fit bead over spiny tip of artichoke. Cut ribbon into 27-inch lengths. Tie ribbon around rim of pot, anchoring in place with hot glue. Tie streamers into bows, bending loops and streamers for a dramatic effect.

PINECONE CHRISTMAS TREES
MAKES 1

❖

urn a pinecone upside down and you have nature's most obvious Christmas ornament. Pinecones look just like little pine trees! With cans of green spray paint and flocking, you can transform a basket of pinecones into a miniature forest. They can be hung from the tree or used in a Christmas scene under the tree (complete with a train). If desired, they can be decorated with dried bittersweet berries or beads.

3-inch to 5-inch pinecones (cones should have opened up enough to stand on their base)
forest green or spruce spray paint
spray flocking
aluminum foil
fine gauge floral wire (if hanging cones from tree)
dried bittersweet berries or colored beads (optional)
toothpicks
thick craft glue

Stand cones on a sheet of foil and spray cones with a light coat of green paint. Allow to dry and repeat with several coats of paint until

pinecones are evenly covered. Spray cones with a very light coat of flocking. If desired, decorate cones with bittersweet berries or beads applied with craft glue and a toothpick. To hang cones from a tree: Cut 8-inch lengths of floral wire. Twish the center of each wire around tip of the pinecone core. Take ends of wire and wrap around tree branch.

CINN-A-MEN WREATH
MAKES 1

❖

This spicy, fragrant paste of cinnamon and applesauce dries into wonderful holiday decorations. You cut it out just as you would cookie dough. Normally I decorate gingerbread men with royal icing (a mixture of egg whites and powdered sugar), but I find these last longer when I pipe white dimensional paint out of a tube. These aren't intended for consumption, and even a trained eye has a hard time telling paint and icing apart. If you're making a large quantity of wreaths for a bazaar, don't go broke buying cinnamon from the supermarket. Check out your local restaurant supplier or wholesale club, where you can buy spices by the gallon. Remember to hang this wreath indoors; a soaking rain or snow will soften the cinn-a-men.

1 cup ground cinnamon
3/4 cup smooth applesauce
mixing bowl
rubber or plastic gloves
wooden board or marble slab
rolling pin
2-inch gingerbread-man cutter
heavy cardboard
floral wire
hot glue gun
tube of white dimensional paint
red and white homespun fabric
12- to 14-inch evergreen wreath

Combine cinnamon and applesauce in bowl. Using gloved hands, mix and knead until smooth. Roll out to 1/4-inch thickness and cut about 12 or 13 figures with cookie cutter. Allow cinn-a-men to dry out for 3 days on cardboard. Cut 8-inch lengths of floral wire and bend in half. Anchor folded ends of wire to backs of figures with hot glue (Fig. 1). Turn right side up and outline with

Fig. 1

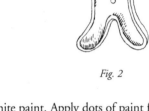

Fig. 2

Fig. 3

white paint. Apply dots of paint for eyes and buttons; make small mark for mouth (Fig. 2). Tear homespun along grain into ³/₄-inch × 8-inch strips. Tie homespun strips into bows. Hold ends of wire together and slip through bows. (Fig. 3). Wire cinn-a-men to wreath (Fig. 4).

Fig. 4

HONEYBEE POTPOURRI WREATHS
MAKES 2

❖

Honey-sweet beeswax has a historically "semiprecious" status. Beeswax candles were treasured by early American settlers and are still among the finest made. Even now, beeswax makes exquisite ornaments when blended with dried flowers and essential oils. Finding the wax at an economical price can be somewhat challenging, but it's well worth the effort. First check your directory to see if there are any beekeepers in your area. Some mail-order crafts suppliers also sell beeswax at a reasonable price. Melting down candles is another option. But whatever the source, beeswax must first be melted down and strained for purity. There are a variety of molds to choose from. Flexible molds designed for casting chocolate are by far the easiest to use, but rigid molds also work, depending upon the design. This project is based on my extensive collection of miniature gelatin ring molds. Why do I have so many? Well, I inherited them from my grandmother. They're not actually antiques—circa 1965 is more like it. Back then, dishes like tomato aspic were considered chic and de rigueur at any dinner party. Too bad . . . I still like aspic salads but I'm embarrassed to serve them to company. Thanks to those trendy "food police," I now keep my gelatin recipes in the closet along with my ring molds. Once a year I pull them out to make holiday decorations, and it always brings back memories of Sunday dinner at Grandma's.

saucepan
2 coffee cans
natural beeswax blocks or candles
paraffin (may be added to extend beeswax)
stocking or leg from pantyhose
ring molds
nonstick cooking spray
dried rose petals and assorted small flowers

essential oils (rose, lavender, vanilla, orange, or cinnamon)
cotton swab
natural jute cord
safety pin
masking tape
two colors of 1/8-inch satin ribbon: 1 foot of each color for each wreath

Opposite: Indian Corn Doll, page 84

Before you begin working with wax, I want to emphasize an important safety factor: WAX IS FLAMMABLE. NEVER MELT IT OVER DIRECT HEAT! A saucepan alone should never be used. While double boilers work well, there's always a slight chance that some wax could drip down the side and onto the burner. For this reason, I'm suggesting that you create a safe double boiler effect. Place a coffee can in a much wider saucepan containing 3 inches of water. Bring water to simmer over medium heat. Add broken pieces of beeswax to can. You may extend the beeswax with blocks of plain paraffin, but do not let it exceed 25% of the mixture. When wax is clear and melted, stretch stocking (or leg of pantyhose) over top of second coffee can. Carefully pour wax through stocking to strain.

Meanwhile, prepare molds. Coat lightly with nonstick cooking spray and wipe off any excess. Combine flowers and rose petals and place a thick layer around bottoms of ring molds. Remelt wax in hot water. Carefully pour wax over flowers in mold. Tap molds lightly on counter to release air pockets. When wax has cooled to opaque state, place molds briefly in freezer. When completely hardened, wax will draw away from sides of molds. Lightly tap molds, inverting into the palm of your hand. Rub surface of molds with cotton swab dipped in the essential oil of your choice.

Hang wreaths by braiding jute with ribbon. To make enough braid for 3 wreaths, cut jute cord and two colors of ribbon into 1-yard lengths. Tie a knot at one end. Thread safety pin through knot and close the pin in a drawer or cabinet door that will stay shut. (You need something that will anchor the thin pin in place as you braid.) Braid jute and ribbon; finish ends with a knot. Divide into 3 equal sections with masking tape (Figs. 1 and 2). Cut between masking tape and tie in knots just above taped ends. Remove tape from ends. Tie braids in a loop through each wax ring, tying in a knot (Fig. 3).

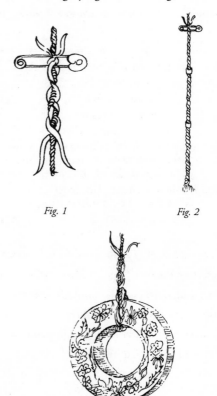

Fig. 1   Fig. 2

Fig. 3

Opposite: Pinecone Table Turkeys, page 99

SILVER BELL SCALLOP SHELLS
MAKES 6

◆

These simple ornaments are simply elegant. I collect small scallop shells just for this purpose. You could use larger ones, but the size of the jingle bells should be adjusted accordingly. You could even spray them gold, which is also quite attractive, but silver is in keeping with the classic Christmas carol. The only trick to making these is in matching up shells. You want to select pairs that are as close in size and shape as possible. Look for shells at crafts suppliers, fish markets, or the beach. Shells sold in most cookware shops for coquilles St-Jacques tend to be on the large side. These instructions are for a half dozen, but if you're going to a bazaar, you'd better make a lot more!

1 dozen small (1- to 1¾-inch) scallop shells
drill with ⅛-inch bit
aluminum foil
silver spray paint
six ½-inch jingle bells
about 3 yards ⅛-inch satin ribbon (I like to use a color that complements the interior of the shell, such as shell pink or mauve)
about 3 yards 1-inch ecru lace (edges of lace should be the same—a mirror image)

Fig. 1

Think of each shell as a fan and drill hole about ¼ inch from the base (Fig. 1). Place shells, with cavities facing down, on aluminum foil. Spray with two coats of spray paint, allowing paint to dry between coats. (If holes clog with paint, clear with a needle.) Cut ribbon and lace into 12 pieces each, about 9 inches in length. Select shell pairs that are most evenly matched in shape and size. String each set of shells with a bell in the center (Fig. 2). Tie ribbon tightly in

Fig. 2

a knot (Fig. 3). Fold lace in a Z, making 3 layers, 3 inches in length. Center bundle of lace over shell and tie with a knot in the ribbon.

Tie another knot 2 inches from lace, forming a hanging loop. Tie ribbon ends in a bow (Fig. 4).

Fig. 3

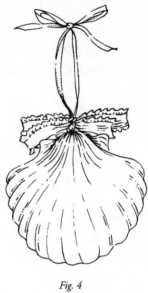

Fig. 4

BAKER'S CLAY CHRISTMAS TREES
MAKES 10 TO 12

❖

*T*his *traditional recipe for faux cookie dough is very versatile. It can be rolled and cut into shapes, or molded like clay. For these ornaments, a garlic press is used to create Christmas trees.*

2¹/₃ cups bleached all-purpose flour
1 cup salt
mixing bowl
1 cup water
red and green paste food coloring
plastic wrap
baking sheet
aluminum foil
garlic press
5 or 6 whole cinnamon sticks, broken in half
floral wire
cooling rack
matte spray acrylic sealer
1 yard ¹/₈-inch red grosgrain ribbon
scissors

Combine flour and salt in mixing bowl. Blend in water and beat or knead to form smooth dough.

Remove ¹/₄ cup dough and tint red. Tint remaining dough green. Wrap red dough in plastic wrap while making trees. Line large baking sheet with foil. Push green dough through garlic press and drop shreds of dough onto foil. Form shreds into ten to twelve 6-inch tree shapes (Fig. 1).

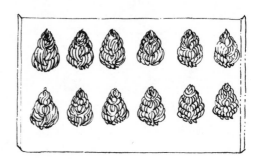

Fig. 1

Push cinnamon stick into base of each tree to form trunk. Cut 4-inch pieces of floral wire and twist into loop (Fig. 2). Push ends of loops into

Fig. 2

treetops. Shape red dough into tiny balls about the size of pearls. Press into trees to resemble ornaments. Bake at 200°F (100°C) for 45 minutes. Cool. Gently remove trees from foil and place on cooling rack. Place cooling rack on baking sheet and bake an additional 30 minutes. Cool. Spray trees with two coats of acrylic sealer, back and front, allowing each coat to dry. Cut ribbon into eight 4¹/₂-inch lengths. Tie a bow around base of loop at the top of each tree (Fig. 3).

Fig. 3

CORNSTARCH CASTING CLAY FOR COOKIE MOLDS
MAKES ABOUT TWELVE 3-INCH × 4-INCH PLAQUES

❖

I've been intrigued with cookie molds ever since I was a little girl. It all started on a family vacation to Colonial Williamsburg. After a tour of the town, I decided that the bakery was the best place to be. My parents kept bringing me back for "just one more ginger cookie." Before we left, I begged them to buy me a pewter gingerbread man mold. It looked more like an eighteenth-century aristocrat in a powdered wig than my idea of a gingerbread boy, and Mom ended up hanging it on the wall. That was the first of my collection. A few years later I slipped into Dad's workshop on a rainy afternoon. I took out all his chisels and mallets and tried making my own molds out of scraps from two-by-fours. I carved witches and ghosts for Halloween, Santas and angels for Christmas, bunnies and ducks for Easter. Dad's workshop was a mess.

It was a few more years until I finally figured out how to get cookies out of the molds. Obviously, the dough wasn't baked in the molds. (The pewter gingerbread man had already come off the wall and been scorched in the oven!) There had to be another way. I researched recipes for shortbread, springerle, and lebkuchen and realized that the molds are only used for imprinting the dough, which is then baked on a cookie sheet. I became particularly interested in beautiful old-world Bavarian molds, not just for cookies but for the decorative plaques that were cast from them. These non-edible works of art are made from a porcelainlike clay of cornstarch. After drying, the relief designs are hand-painted and hung up on the wall. If you don't have any cookie molds (collector's quality molds can be pricey), plastic chocolate molds work equally well. Terracotta cookie molds are also widely available in cookware departments and specialty kitchen shops.

1 cup cornstarch
2 cups baking soda
1 1/3 cups cold water
large plate
damp cloth
pastry board or butcher block
pastry cloth with rolling pin cover
rolling pin
cookie or chocolate mold(s)
ice pick (for punching holes) or
thin copper wire (for hanging loops)
cooling racks
acrylic paint or watercolors
(colors to suit design)
small detail paintbrushes
matte or gloss spray acrylic sealer

Combine cornstarch and baking soda in small saucepan. Blend in water with wire whisk. Heat, whisking constantly, until mixture is the consistency of mashed potatoes. Turn out on large plate and cover with damp cloth until cool enough to handle. Knead until smooth on board dusted with cornstarch. Dust pastry cloth and rolling pin cover with additional cornstarch. Roll out dough to desired thickness (usually 1/2 inch) and imprint with mold, trimming around edges. Poke hole in top of each plaque with ice pick, or make a loop with 3-inch piece of wire, ends twisted together and pressed into center top edge of casting. Place plaques on cooling racks and allow to air dry completely for about 2 weeks. (Do not put in oven; they will crack.) Paint relief of designs as desired. Spray both front and back with several coats of acrylic sealer, allowing it to dry between coats. (This will prevent humidity or bugs from damaging castings in the years to come.)

Plaques and ornaments molded in this fashion make popular items for holiday bazaars. They're perfect for home decorating, tree trimming and unique Christmas gifts.

(Continued)

Opposite: Bay Leaf Spice Wreath, page 101

SCOTTIE TREE SKIRT
MAKES 1

❖

I *once knew the dearest little Scottish terrier named Duchess. During the holidays her owners,* *our next-door neighbors, would dress her in a big red bow with bells around her neck. She'd* *come trotting down the snowy street, looking like she'd just stepped off the cover of a greeting* *card. Scotties are the quintessential Christmas dog. They look great with plaid. No wonder you* *see them on everything from sweaters to shortbread tins.*

Poor Duchess drowned one summer in Long Island Sound. She fell off a boat dock in the harbor. I *still think of her around Christmastime, and her memory inspired my favorite tree skirt.*

3 yards 54-inch plaid wool flannel
(Royal Stewart or Black Watch tartan)
tape measure
chalk
scissors
1/3 yard 54- to 60-inch black wool felt
pins
sewing machine
glue stick (or fusible web)
5 yards 1 1/2- to 2-inch black wool or
cotton fringe
five 1-inch brass buttons with crest
black and red thread, needle
1 1/3 yards 5/8-inch red grosgrain ribbon
eighteen 3/8-inch brass jingle bells
6 white shirt buttons
black embroidery floss

Cut plaid flannel into 1 1/2-yard sections. Cut into two 54-inch-diameter circles. The best way to do this is to fold fabric in quarters. Find the center corner and use that as a radiating point. Using a tape measure, mark a chalk line 27 inches from radiating point (Fig. 1). Cut through all

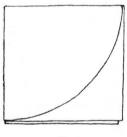

Fig. 1

thicknesses. Cut 8-inch hole in center. Cut second piece of flannel to match the first. Cut a slit through both circles, running from outer edge to center hole (Fig. 2). Enlarge Scottie pattern to

(Continued)

Opposite: Cinn-a-men Wreath, page 104

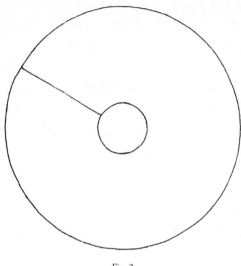

Fig. 2

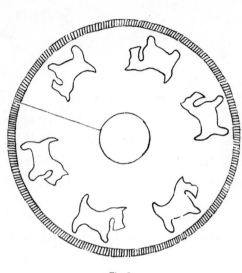

Fig. 3

scale. Pin onto wool felt and cut out 6 figures. Arrange Scotties evenly on right side of one plaid circle, all facing in same direction. Use glue stick or fusible web to bond them in place. Appliqué Scotties to flannel using a sewing machine. This can be done in one of two ways: carefully sew around black felt 1/8 inch from edge, using straight stitch, or use zigzag satin stitch about 3/8 inch wide to completely overcast felt edges. Pin fringe around outer edge of plaid circle, with fringe facing in. Baste in place (Fig. 3). Pin second plaid circle right side down over Scotties. Sew around all edges using 1/2-inch seam, leaving a 12-inch opening at edge of circle to turn. Clip curves (Fig. 4). Turn fabric and press. Topstitch fabric 1/4 inch from edge all around outer edge, side openings, and inner circle. Make 5 evenly spaced 1 1/4-inch button holes down one side of opening. Sew corresponding

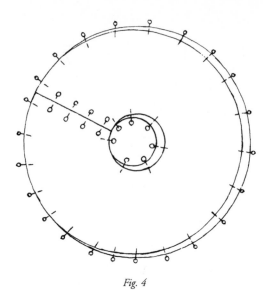

Fig. 4

Fig. 5

brass buttons to opposite side. Cut ribbon into 4-inch lengths. Tie 6 pieces into bows. Pin remaining pieces across Scotties' necks, doubling ends back underneath ribbon. Slipstitch in place. Stitch bow to collar at nape of neck. Stitch 3 bells along each collar, sewing through all thicknesses of fabric (this helps keep layers from slipping). Sew one shirt button on each face for an eye, using thick shank of embroidery floss to look like a pupil. Sew buttons through all thicknesses of fabric (Fig. 5).

(Continued)

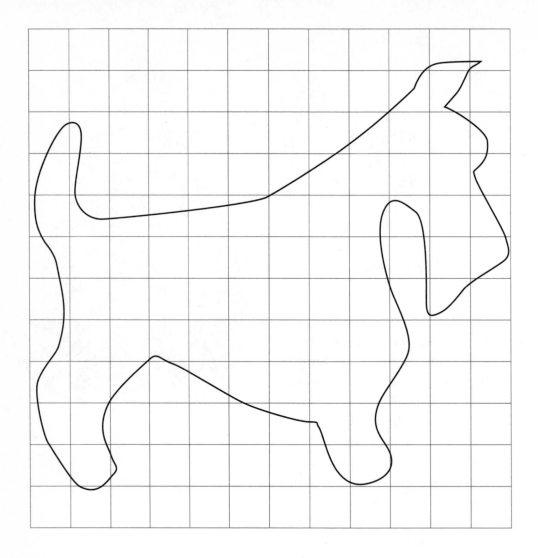

1 square = 1 inch

Necktie Teddy
MAKES 1

❖

Necktie teddies make cute little stocking stuffers or tree ornaments. Children absolutely adore them, as do adults. Sometimes I'll fill these with potpourri and use them for drawer sachets. I keep a large bag of discarded ties in the attic just for such projects. Stains aren't a problem because you can always cut around them. Patterns, though, can be a problem, especially with unusual or trendy ties. The most effective ties for this purpose are the classics: stripes, dots, paisleys, and small preppy prints. Keep in mind that extremely narrow ties are difficult to work with.

wide necktie, seam ripper, or ¼-yard
necktie fabric
paper
fabric marker
pins
scissors
needle
thread to match tie
sewing machine
cotton or polyester stuffing
black embroidery floss
³/₈-inch black shoe button
scrap of ¼-inch satin ribbon in color
to coordinate with tie

Carefully take necktie apart with seam ripper. Press out seams so that material lies flat. (If using necktie fabric, skip this step.) Copy pattern pieces onto paper and cut out. Pin pieces to the fabric on the straight edge of the grain. Draw around pieces with fabric marker. You'll need: 2 body-head pieces, 2

Fig. 1

muzzle pieces, and 4 arm, leg, and ear pieces. DO NOT CUT MARKED FABRIC. Instead, satin-stich around outline using the fine zig-zap setting on sewing machine (Fig. 1). Trim fabric close to stitched edges. Pin ears, right sides together, whipstitch around edges, and turn (Fig. 2).

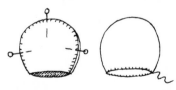

Fig. 2

(Continued)

Position ears on one of the body-head pieces. Baste in place (Fig. 3). Pin remaining body-head

Fig. 3

piece right side down. Whipstitch around edges, leaving a 1-inch opening at the side to turn. Turn and stuff, slipstitching opening (Fig. 4). Pin arms and legs together and whipstitch around edges, leaving open ends to turn. Turn and stuff (Fig. 5). Tuck open edges of fabric under, and slipstitch arms and legs onto body-head section. Pin muzzle pieces right sides together and whipstitch around edges, leaving

Fig. 4

a 1/2-inch opening at the side to turn. Turn and lightly stuff with a pinch of stuffing (do not overstuff muzzle). Whipstitch muzzle onto bear's face, around edges. Use black embroidery floss

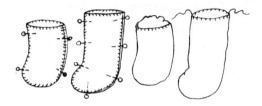

Fig. 5

to stitch button onto center of muzzle for nose, pulling through both layers of muzzle, anchoring to the face. Use floss to stitch 2 small dots for eyes. Tie a small necktie around bear with a piece of satin ribbon (Fig. 6). If you're using these as ornaments, make loop of ribbon and stitch to top of head.

Fig. 6

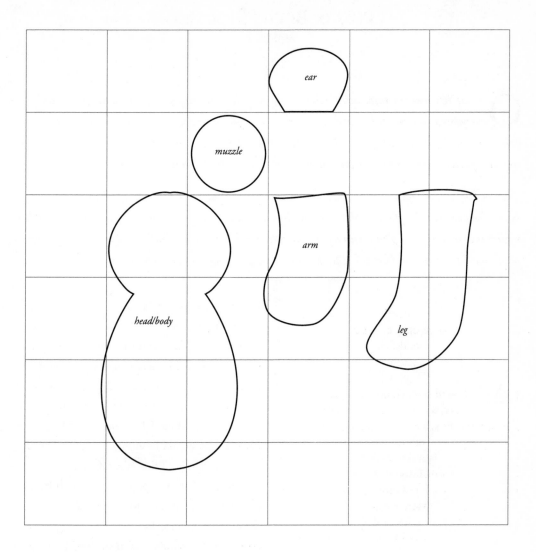

1 square = 1 inch

Puss in Boots Stocking
MAKES 1

❖

*O*ur cat Itty was my inspiration for this project. Her curiosity gets her into anything and everything. Whenever I hear a suspicious noise, bump, rattle, or rustle I don't automatically call 911—first I call, "Here, Kitty Kitty!" Her little gray head then pops up out of the most unlikely places. Those green eyes look at me as if to ask, "What's **your** problem?"

This stocking is really quite simple, since it's constructed from felt. The cat's face is glued to the stocking back. The front panel is glued in place and finished with a decorative overcast stitch (and a yarn ball). I recommend making paw prints with a black laundry marker. Once I actually tried using some fabric paint and Itty's own John Hancock. But she's a very busy cat and left her signature on more than the felt!

pencil
large sheet of paper
yardstick
scissors
pins
$1/2$ yard 60-inch off-white felt
5-inch square of light gray felt
scraps of light yellow-green and light pink felt
fabric glue
laundry marker
$3/4$-inch styrofoam ball
red yarn
yarn needle
index card
craft knife
stencil brush
black cream-style stencil paint
small brass ring
needle
off-white thread

Enlarge patterns to scale, using yardstick for guide. Cut back and front of stocking from off-white felt. Cut head and paws of cat from gray felt. (Cut paws from scraps after cutting around head.) Cut eyes from scraps of green and nose from scrap of pink felt. Line up edges of cat head with top of felt fabric backing. Glue in place. Edges should be even with each other; if not, trim slightly so they meet. Glue eyes and nose in position. Add pupils to eyes with laundry marker; use marker to outline eyes and define nose, mouth, and ears (Fig. 1). Pipe thin bead of glue around edges of stocking backing. Align front panel on backing and press along glued seams. Position gray felt paws halfway above upper edge of front panel and glue in place (Fig. 2). Allow to dry. Cover styrofoam ball

Opposite: Silver Bell Scallop Shells, page 108

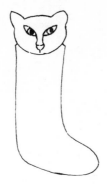

Fig. 1

Fig. 3

Fig. 2

design onto index card. Cut out pattern with craft knife to make stencil. Hold stencil firmly against felt. Coat end of stencil brush with paint and "pounce" brush up and down over stencil. Lift card straight up so as not to smear paint. Repeat, making paw prints in "walking" pattern (Fig. 4) going up stocking. Sew ring to back of stocking at the top of head. Use to hang stocking from mantle.

with glue. Wind enough yarn around ball to look like a yarn ball. Make a knot 6 inches from ball and unwind enough yarn to sew around stocking. Thread needle with yarn ball at opposite end; the knot will be your starting point. Pull yarn through upper left edge of stocking until knot reaches eye of needle. Begin overcasting around stocking, about $1/4$ inch from edge (Fig. 3). Finish with knot at upper right edge. To make paw prints, transfer paw print

Fig. 4

(Continued)

Opposite: Necktie Teddy, page 119

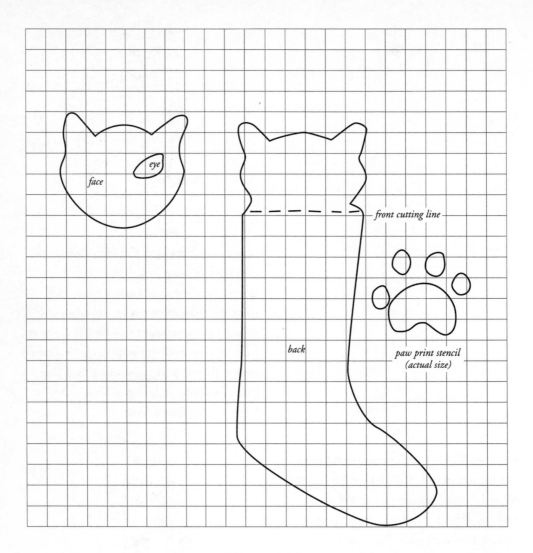

face

eye

front cutting line

back

*paw print stencil
(actual size)*

1 square = 1 inch

ROVER WREATH
MAKES 1

❖

*T*hese days, you see more and more canine crafts at holiday bazaars. "Dog people" just can't resist picking something up for their favorite family member. Believe me, I know. I have nine! Around our house, we buy dog biscuits by the bushel. This door ornament evolved naturally.

10-inch styrofoam ring (3/4-inch thick
with 8-inch hole)
2-inch bone-shaped dog biscuits
(approximately 48 to 56)
hot glue gun
gold or silver spray paint
aluminum foil
2 1/2 yards 3/4-inch plaid ribbon
thick craft glue
gold plated, brass, or silver dog tags
(match to paint)
floral wire
picture hanging loop

Use glue gun to attach about 2 dozen biscuits around wreath. Biscuits should touch at inner edge of wreath and spread slightly at outer edge (Fig. 1).

Fig. 1

Hot glue a second layer of biscuits on top of first layer so that they overlap, covering any spaces. Place wreath on foil and spray with several coats of paint, allowing to dry between coats. Use craft glue to apply ribbon around the outer and inner edges of the styrofoam ring. Make a double-loop bow out of the remaining ribbon. Hot glue layers together in center, and wrap center with a 2-inch piece of ribbon, giving at the back. Wire dog tags into the center of the bow (Fig. 2) with a small piece of floral wire.

Fig. 2

Hot glue bow along side of wreath (Fig. 3). Hot glue picture hanging loop to the back of wreath.

Fig. 3

NUTCRACKER CHRISTMAS BOX
MAKES 1

❖

Thisis handsome box is a keepsake gift in its own right, although I've used it as a special container to present jewelry, airline tickets, or certificates. I use mine year after year as a vessel for spicy potpourri. If you intend to make a box for this purpose, it's important to drill holes around the sides, allowing the aroma to escape. For the perfect potpourri, try using the recipe from **Cinnamon Sachet Apples** *(page 65)*. I think the smell of cinnamon sparks holiday memories—as well as an appetite for autumn apple pies. The size of the box really depends on what you plan to put inside. As holiday bazaar items, these are popular when used for the most obvious application . . . pistachio nuts. After all, you've already cracked open the shells to glue on top! Wrap them in food safe cellophane, add a gold seal, and you have a gourmet gift.

oval Shaker wood box (5 to 9 inches long)
drill with 1/8-inch bit (optional)
sandpaper
ivy or forest green wood stain
rag
aluminum foil
matte spray acrylic sealer
natural or red unsalted pistachios
nutcracker
thick craft glue
toothpaste
plaid ribbon (width of box lid band
and circumference of band + 1 inch)
scroll saw
cinnamon stick

OPTIONAL FILLINGS:
CINNAMON-SCENTED POTPOURRI (page 67), or
pistachios, clear cellophane, gold seal, or
small gifts, accessories, or papers of value

If you will be filling box with potpourri, drill holes at 1-inch intervals around box, about 1/3 inch below lid line with lid in place.

Sand outside and inside surfaces of box lid and base until smooth. Stain green both outside and inside for potpourri or gift box. (Just stain outside for pistachio nut box.) Allow stain to dry. Place box on aluminum foil and apply a coat of spray sealer. Allow to dry. Crack pistachios open, saving shells that haven't been split or damaged by the nutcracker. (Reserve nutmeats to fill box, or for other uses.) Practice lining up shells in the shape of a triangular tree. Once you have the desired shape laid out (Fig. 1), glue in place with craft glue. (Use sparingly, applying around rims of shells with toothpick. Excess glue will ooze out

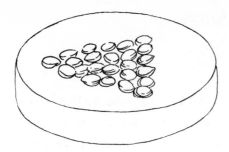

Fig. 1

from under shells and look sloppy.) Glue ribbon around lid of box, doubling back end and tucking under (Fig. 2). Use scroll saw to cut

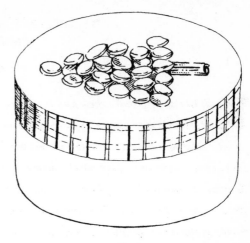

Fig. 3

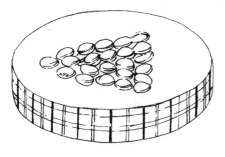

Fig. 2

cinnamon stick the length of a "tree trunk" in proportion to the tree and box. Glue in place (Fig. 3). Apply a second coat of spray acrylic sealer to lid. Fill box with potpourri or wrap shelled pistachios in squares of cellophane, place in box, and secure with gold seal.

STUFFED SOCK SNOWMEN
MAKES 2

❖

Kids love to help make these and line them up on a windowsill or across the fireplace mantel. It's important to use the right kind of socks. You'll need white tube-style terry socks, or athletic socks that have a fleecy nap on the inside. In either case, there should be no knitted-in heels. For stocking caps, use a similar pair of red socks and a pom-pom. These snowmen are designed somewhat like punching bag dummies. The bottoms are weighted down with aquarium gravel or dried split peas. While you're whipping some up, why stop at one pair? Stuff a whole family of snowmen for your next holiday bazaar!

10- to 12-inch terry tube socks
(1 pair white, 1 pair red)
cotton or polyester stuffing
elastic cord
scissors
plastic wrap
aquarium gravel (or dried split peas)
2 rubber bands
pins
needle
thread (white, red, black)
1-inch white or green pom-pom
sixteen 3/8-inch black shoe buttons
two 1-inch × 12-inch strips of red
tartan plaid wool

Fig. 1

heights of your snowmen. Tear off a square of plastic wrap for each sock. Place about 2/3 cup gravel or peas in center of each square. Gather up

Turn white socks nap side out. Fill about 4 inches of toe with stuffing. Tie tightly with piece of elastic cord, trimming off ends of elastic (Fig. 1). Turn cuff of each sock up into body from 2 to 3 1/2 inches (Fig. 2); you may want to vary the

Fig. 2

edges of plastic and secure with rubber band. Trim off gathered plastic (Fig. 3). Encase gravel pouches

Fig. 3

in wads of stuffing like big snowballs (Fig. 4). Stuff into lower bodies of snowmen. Pin bottoms

Fig. 4

together, tucking in at each corner. Slipstitch bottoms closed with white thread (Fig. 5).

Fig. 5

Turn red socks nap side out. Gather about half-way between toe and cuff. Tie with a piece of elastic cord. Trim off toe above elastic (Fig. 6). Turn socks and secure gathered ends with some

Fig. 6

stitches of red thread. Roll up cuffs until stocking caps are desired length (Fig. 7). Slipstitch stocking caps to head and sew pom-pom on gathered end

Fig. 7

of cap. Sew buttons on face and body: 2 for eyes, 3 for mouth, and 3 buttons. Tie plaid wool around necks for scarves. Trim ends to desired length and unravel slightly for fringe (Fig. 8).

Fig. 8

BE MINE ROSEBUDS
MAKES 12

❖

I've always been in love with dried roses. On Valentine's Day I'd rather receive a dozen of these than a bouquet of fresh ones. Perhaps it's just my nature—I can't bear to watch beautiful things die. I once went so far as to take a delivery of sweetheart roses from the doorstep and, instead of putting them in a vase, immediately hang them upside down in the pantry to dry. Some people would consider that a sacrilege, but I still have those roses!

A single well-preserved rose is really quite special. One of the best ways to set it off is in a miniature flowerpot. Standing solitaire, surrounded by Spanish moss, it reminds me of a tiny topiary tree. Make several dozen if you're bringing these to a bazaar. They're the perfect impulse/gift item and they disappear in minutes.

1 dozen dried roses or rosebuds
floral oasis
craft knife
1 dozen miniature 1¹/₂-inch flower pots
thick craft glue
Spanish moss
2 yards ¹/₂-inch ruffled ecru lace
3 yards ¹/₈-inch satin ribbon
(in color to match roses)
nail

Fig. 1

Trim rose stems to about 2¹/₂ to 3 inches. Cut floral oasis into small cubes that will fit into flowerpots. Apply some glue around insides of pots and push foam inside. Pinch off clumps of Spanish moss and glue to tops of foam (Fig. 1). Cut lace into about 6-inch lengths. (Miniature pots vary but the circumference is usually 5¹/₂ inches.) Apply thin line of glue around rim of pots and glue lace around rim. Cut ribbon into twelve 6-inch lengths and twelve 3-inch lengths. Glue 6-inch strips of ribbon around rim of pots at upper edge of lace (Fig. 2). Tie 3-inch lengths

Opposite: Be Mine Rosebuds, page 130

Fig. 2

into 12 small bows. Glue in place over seam of
ribbon on pot. Poke nail into oasis through
moss. (Prepunching holes helps prevent breaking
rose stems.) Dip stems into glue and insert roses
into holes (Fig. 3).

Fig. 3

Opposite: Sweetheart Sachets, page 132
With Rose Petal Potpourri, page 135

SWEETHEART SACHETS
MAKES 4

❖

*A*long with a box of chocolates or a dozen roses, sweetheart sachets are a classic Valentine's *gift. This ever popular country bazaar item is easy to make. You can concoct your own rose petal potpourri or buy it prepackaged.*

1/4 yard pink satin moiré or brocade
21/2 yards 1-inch ruffled ecru lace
pins
needle
thread
ROSE PETAL POTPOURRI (instructions follow)
3/4 yard 1/4-inch pink or ecru satin ribbon
41/2-inch satin roses

Cut 8 hearts out of fabric, approximately 3 inches high and 31/4 inches wide. (After cutting one heart, use it as pattern to cut out the rest.) For each sachet: Place fabric right side up. Line up

selvage of lace with edge of heart and pin in place, beginning at center (Fig. 1). Baste lace in place about 1/4 inch from edge of fabric. Place

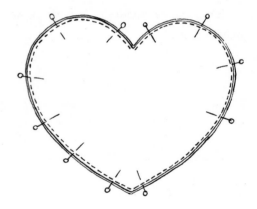

Fig. 1

another fabric heart right side down over lace and pin in place. Stitch around heart, leaving 1-inch opening to turn fabric (Fig. 2). Remove pins and turn fabric right side out through opening. Stuff heart with potpourri and slipstitch opening. Cut ribbon into four 6-inch pieces. Cross ends of ribbon at center of heart and tack in place. Stitch rose on top (Fig. 3).

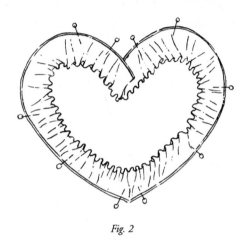

Fig. 2

Fig. 3

(Continued)

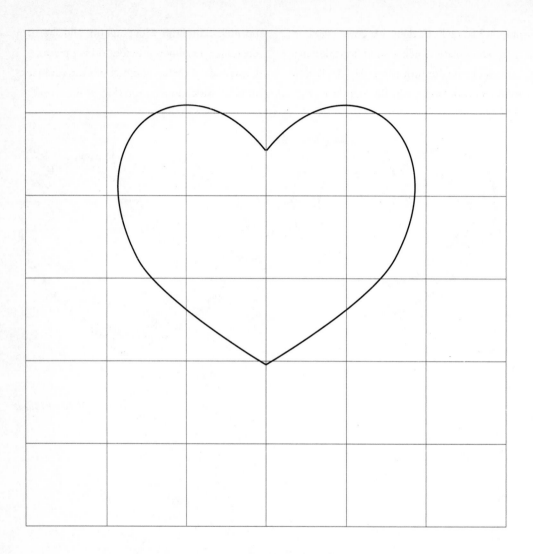

1 square = 1 inch

Rose Petal Potpourri
MAKES ABOUT 2¹/₂ CUPS

2 cups dried rose petals
2 dozen dried eucalyptus leaves, crushed
1 dozen dried sage leaves, crushed
3 dried rosemary stems, crushed
1 teaspoon orrisroot powder*
4 to 5 drops concentrated rose oil

Toss together and store in airtight jar or container. Makes enough to fill about 10 sachets.

NOTE: Look for orrisroot powder at a nursery or crafts store or in the floral department of a supermarket.

INDEX

———— ❖ ————